D1541429

# THE ACCOUNTANT'S STRATEGIC MARKETING GUIDE

CAROLE A. CONGRAM

RUTH J. DUMESIC

**JOHN WILEY & SONS**
New York • Chichester • Brisbane • Toronto • Singapore

***Library of Congress Cataloging in Publication Data:***

The accountant's strategic marketing guide.

Includes index.
1. Accounting—Marketing. I. Congram, Carole A.
II. Dumesic, Ruth J. III. Title.

HF5657.A256 1986     657'.068'8     86-9065
ISBN   0-471-84732-1

Printed in the United States of America

10   9   8   7   6   5   4   3   2   1

# CONTRIBUTORS

**Maureen Broderick**
Manager—Professional Services Marketing
Price Waterhouse, San Francisco

**Robert W. Denney**
President
Robert Denney Associates, Wayne, Pennsylvania

**Michael F. Dunleavy**
Director of Marketing Development
KMG Main Hurdman, National Office, New York

**Susan M. Fryer**
Director of Communications
Peat Marwick, St. Louis

**Mary S. Hinkel**
Director of Marketing
Touche Ross, Atlanta

**Peter M. Horowitz**
National Director of Marketing
Coopers & Lybrand, Toronto, Canada

**Robert J. Killian**
Vice President
Bozell, Jacobs, Kenyon & Eckhardt, Chicago

**John T. Schiffman**
Partner
Smith Batchelder & Rugg, Hanover, New Hampshire

**Pamela N. Terry**
Consultant, Houston

**Bernard E. Ury**
President
Bernard E. Ury Associates, Inc., Chicago

**Kent Wheiler**
Graduate School of Business
The University of Texas at Austin

# FOREWORD

Today is truly an exciting time for marketing. I have been, for the last 15 years, a marketing professor, a marketing researcher, a marketing author, and a marketing consultant. At no time have I seen more interest in marketing than is evident right now. I think that the high level of interest in marketing is happening in three dimensions.

The first dimension is the rediscovery of marketing in older, well-established organizations. Managers in these organizations are now recalling that being close to the marketplace, being sensitive to the client, is the way to compete in world and domestic markets of the 1980s.

Secondly, I see a growing interest in marketing at our colleges and universities.

The third dimension is particularly relevant to the readers of this book. Marketing's increased importance can be seen in emerging interest areas, which would include, of course, services marketing and, particularly, the marketing of professional services. This new dimension has arisen because of deregulation, increasing competition, and changing customer or client bases of organizations such as represented by many of the readers of this book.

Marketing's profile—marketing's importance in this country,

and, actually, around the world—has never been higher. It is within this context that a quality book on the marketing of accounting services is so timely. Although marketing's value should not be oversold, its relevance is quickly becoming recognized by astute accounting professionals. Given this awareness, this book will fill an obvious need and will undoubtedly serve as a stimulus to additional contributions.

In closing, I want to express appreciation to both Carole Congram and Ruth Dumesic for the quality and extent of their effort in preparing this valuable book. It represents a permanent and substantial contribution to an emerging area of accounting and marketing interest. Thank you, Carole and Ruth.

STEPHEN W. BROWN

*President of*
*American Marketing*
*Association 1984–1985*
*Professor and Director of*
*First Interstate Center for Services Marketing*
*Arizona State University*
*Tempe, Arizona*

# PREFACE

When managers speak of marketing, they usually mean the organized performance of all *selling* functions. This is still selling. It still
starts out with "our products." It still looks for "our market." True
marketing starts out the way Sears starts out—with the customer,
his demographics, his realities, his needs, his values. It does not ask,
"What do we want to sell?" It asks, "What does the customer want to
buy?" It does not say, "This is what our product or service does." It
says, "These are the satisfactions the customer looks for, values, and
needs."

Indeed, selling and marketing are antithetical rather than synony-
mous or even complementary.

There will always, one can assume, be need for some selling. But the
aim of marketing is to make selling superfluous. The aim of marketing is to know and understand the customer so well that the product
or service fits him and sells itself.

Ideally, marketing should result in a customer who is ready to buy.

Peter F. Drucker

*Management; Tasks,
Responsibilities, Practices*
Harper & Row, 1974, p. 64

To paraphrase Drucker, marketing in an accounting firm
should result in a client who is ready to buy the firm's services.

In a few firms, that is happening; marketing underlies these firms' substantial expansion and growth.

Revenue growth rates of 30 percent to 50 percent annually
New and expanded services to existing clients
Better utilization at all professional levels
Increased recognition among referral sources
Reduced staff turnover
Successful recruiting of top-notch professionals
Increasing market penetration

In the large majority of both large and small firms, however, marketing is a catchword for a series of independent, sales-oriented activities appearing to be beneficial, but yielding mixed results, usually unquantifiable and accompanied by high frustration levels. Why? Most accounting firms start by asking two seemingly simple questions: "What marketing activities have proven successful for accounting firms?" and "Can I use any of them in my firm?"

For example, through a seminar, a firm's professionals believe that they have established the firm's credibility in a specialized area, but the firm has obtained no additional work. Another firm develops a brochure with the expectation of attracting new clients. When business does not expand, they attribute the failure to the brochure, not to the absence of a brochure distribution strategy. Certainly the partners in these firms believe that they have made an investment, sometimes significant in terms of resources expended, but there are no results. Something is missing, but what is it? Why do some firms develop marketing strategies that work—consistently?

The missing ingredient is process. To be successful in marketing, you must invest in a process, not in a series of projects. This process is strategic market planning, in which you assess the strengths of your firm, identify its unique characteristics, and develop tailored marketing programs that not only set you apart from the competition, but also deliver the results you and your partners want.

Your firm's client orientation and the strategic marketing process are the focal points of our first two chapters. Here we'll discuss why strategic marketing is vital to your firm's success and also describe how you and your partners can adapt the process to your firm.

After you and your partners accept marketing as a process, implementation responsibility will become a major concern. Who is in charge of the marketing program? What resources are needed? How do you manage a public relations consultant? These resource-related questions are the focus of the second section of the book.

The third section focuses on your firm's future. We believe that you can use this volume best in conjunction with your firm's planning activities. If all the partners and professionals in your firm have read this book, they will have a common base for developing a plan that they own, a plan in which they will be involved, and a plan that yields results. Further, once the plan is developed, they will have the background to make intelligent decisions about resource allocations. Then, you will be ready to work on the "how to" of specific marketing tools. Most firms start with them and, thus, become project driven. You must avoid this trap through the strategic marketing process.

Eleven professionals, experienced in the marketing of accounting services, join us in discussing the key factors in strategic marketing. Their works here are based on presentations they made at a symposium, "Success Factors in Marketing Accounting Services." The symposium, which brought together for the first time marketing and accounting professionals, was sponsored by the American Marketing Association and held in Chicago on June 14–15, 1984.

As cochairs of the symposium, we wish to thank Leonard L. Berry (Texas A&M University), Harvey D. Braun (Touche Ross), Gregory D. Upah (Young & Rubicam), and William T. Young (Williams, Young & Associates) for their enthusiastic support of the event; August Aquila (Friedman, Eisenstein, Raemer & Schwartz), Samuel A. Cypert (Peat Marwick), William R. George (Villanova University), Louise A. Myers, and Kent Wheiler (The University of Texas at Austin) for actively participating in the symposium; Susan Morace (Touche Ross) for effective administrative support; Cameron B. Duncan (Touche Ross) for being our utility infielder; and Sharon B. Jochimsen for timely transcription service.

In developing the manuscript for publication, we were fortunate to have so many knowledgeable people willing to help us. We thank Robert J. Bartels, Ronald P. Brotherton, John L. Diesem, Ron Ledwith, and Edwin H. Ruzinsky for their insightful advice and counsel. Jeff Brown, our editor at John Wiley, has been generous in sharing his experience and ideas. We have also benefited from the broad experience of the Wiley production team: Carole Schwager, Melonie Parnes, Maryan Malone, and Mary Daniello. Various parts of the manuscript were reviewed by the contributors, as well as a group of business and professional colleagues: Carl T. Burton, Pamela Cuming, Cameron B. Duncan, William R. George, John F. Mullarkey, Anthony Vlamis, Sharyn Wisniewski, and William T. Young. We cherish you all.

This is an exciting time for all professionals. Shaping the future of your firm demands objectivity, creativity, new perspectives, perseverance, and openness to change. We wish you and your colleagues every success in developing a marketing approach based on service that is truly responsive to the needs of your clients.

CAROLE A. CONGRAM
RUTH J. DUMESIC

*New York, New York*
*Madison, Wisconsin*
*April 1986*

# CONTENTS

# PART ONE

# HOW TO GET STARTED

# 1

## CLIENT-CENTERED FIRMS WIN

1. Is price the principal concern of your firm's current and prospective clients?      Yes      No

2. Do recommendations from current clients represent one of your firm's principal sources of new clients?      Yes      No

3. When you sponsor a seminar for clients and prospective clients in your firm, do you have a follow-up plan in place before the seminar takes place?      Yes      No

4. Do technical practitioners play a role in marketing your firm's services?      Yes      No

5. Does your firm have a client service planning process that works?      Yes      No

The authors appreciate the contributions of Alfred L. McDougal and Paul Munsen, chief executive officers of McDougal, Littell & Company and Munsen's Discovery Enterprises, respectively, to this chapter. The quotations attributed to "a chief executive officer," as well as several examples of service quality, were drawn from their presentations at a symposium, "Success Factors in Marketing Accounting Services," held on June 14–15, 1984, and sponsored by the American Marketing Association.

6. Do your clients frequently receive their reports late because your firm has several review steps?  Yes  No

7. Is the primary purpose of your firm's marketing brochure to describe the firm and its services?  Yes  No

8. Do your professionals understand the concerns and problems of managers in the production and sales areas of a client's organization?  Yes  No

9. Within the past two years, have you hired a third party to survey your clients to find out if they are satisfied with your firm's services?  Yes  No

10. At the completion of your annual audit, does a client CEO receive a letter of recommendations that helps him take action to manage his organization better?  Yes  No

## ☐ WHAT'S YOUR FIRM'S SERVICE ORIENTATION?

To an accounting firm, clients represent a major asset. First, the recurring nature of many services a firm provides to a client makes a stable client base very valuable. Also, the special consultative services and the strong personal ties this recurring work could engender enhance the likelihood of a long-term relationship that is mutually rewarding.

However great the potential, the reality is different. To the dismay of professionals in large and small firms alike, clients seek competitive proposals and shop for low fees. They change accounting firms, sometimes before the old firm knows it has been replaced. They even engage several firms simultaneously, each for a different service.

In response, many firms have discovered "marketing." The usual approach has been to match the various tools (e.g., brochures, seminars, sales training) against selected criteria (e.g., price, ease of production or implementation, personal interest). Then, one or more tools are selected and implemented, frequently with limited results and high frustration. In their eagerness, haste, excitement, or panic, accounting professionals have ignored the successful product-marketing experience and have missed the most important and most informative element in marketing: the client.

Most definitions of *marketing* point to the client or customer as the key to strategy, plans, services, and organization. However, accounting firms have not used client observations and feedback to the firms' advantage. Now you may argue that accountants in professional practice, by definition, have a client focus. After all, a practice cannot exist without clients. We would counter that existence is not enough. In a competitive environment, firms must grow, and continued growth results from market sensitivity. The basic strategic decision you or your firm's management group must make concerns your firm's degree of market sensitivity: *Do we want our firm to be technically oriented or client-centered?* Let's discuss the difference.

## What Is the Focus of the Technically Oriented Firm?

The technically oriented firm revolves around the services its professionals or regulatory agencies define as needed by clients. New services develop from the interests of the firm's professionals, rather than from market needs. Thus, some new services are much more successful than others. Investments in growth-oriented programs and research yielding long-term results are minimal. Communication—largely one-way, from the firm to the client—emphasizes the firm's point of view, with "we" dominating publications, correspondence, proposals, and other communications to clients. The focus of the technically oriented firm is the firm, not the market.

## What Is the Client-Oriented Focus?

The client-centered firm's interaction with its market involves a two-step procedure as a means of achieving growth and profit. An analysis of the client-focused firm will first indicate the frequency with which a firm solicits (directly or through third parties) clients' views on:

1. Services they use currently
2. Their satisfaction with these services
3. Assistance or services they need
4. The image of the firm and its competitors

Second, and more important, is the follow-through procedure which indicates the extent to which the firm incorporates this information into its structure, organization, and operations by:

1. Improving and refining services currently offered
2. Developing new services needed by clients
3. Modifying and reshaping the service delivery process
4. Developing professionals who understand the market
5. Revising or reinforcing the message the firm communicates to the marketplace

In short, the client-centered firm is market driven, and analysis of the client's views is crucial.

## Where Do You Want to Be on the Service Orientation Continuum?

Service orientation is neither black nor white. Rather, it is a continuum on which the technical and the client-centered positions represent the opposite ends. You and your partners must determine where you want your firm to be on the continuum. Today, most firms are oriented toward the technical end, which is understandable, owing to the technical underpinnings of the profession. To remain at the technical end, however, is to survive, at best. The firms that commit to the client-centered end will have the winning edge because they will build the loyal, long-term relationships that come from delivering services that clients need and want. What service orientation do you want your firm to have?

Once you and your partners have decided where you want your firm to be on that continuum, you must evaluate where your firm is today. The gap tells you how far you have to go. The 10 questions that opened this chapter provide a reference point. Partners in the client-centered firm respond:

|     |     |     |     |
| --- | --- | --- | --- |
| 1.  | No  | 6.  | No  |
| 2.  | Yes | 7.  | No  |
| 3.  | Yes | 8.  | Yes |
| 4.  | Yes | 9.  | Yes |
| 5.  | Yes | 10. | Yes |

Give yourself 10 points for every response with which you agreed. If you score 90 or 100, your firm should be winning consistently. This volume will reinforce much of what you know and are doing, and we hope you will find some new ideas.

If you scored 70 or 80, you are having a lot of success, but too frequently you hear, "Your firm was a strong second." If you scored 60 or below, you are not taking advantage of the strengths you and your professionals have worked hard to develop. In fact, your best, most profitable clients are another firm's targets. You cannot afford to miss any more market opportunities if your firm is going to be in existence 10 years from now.

## ☐ THE CLIENT PERSPECTIVE: OR, WHY YOU CAN'T AFFORD TO BE MYOPIC

The idea of asking clients and prospective clients for their opinions about your firm's services is scary. You might not like what you hear. Clients' responses may also indicate needs for changes, requiring that you divert attention and resources. However, you must balance that fear by focusing on what's good, what works. After all, your clients chose your firm for what they considered good reasons. You should know what clients like about your services and delivery systems and capitalize on those points. Probably the best and easiest approach is to view this process as a way to substantiate the impressions that people have developed over the years.

Fortunately, clients agree on the general criteria they use in evaluating firms—while being served as clients or when selecting an accounting firm. Your job is to relate each general criterion to the specific goals and programs of your practice for validation by your firm's clients. In the following three sections, we describe these criteria and relate them to the client-oriented firm. Our sources were a minifocus group, our experiences with professionals, and the research literature. Participating in the minifocus group were two chief executive officers of *Inc.* 500 companies: Alfred L. McDougal and Paul Munsen. The supporting quotations, as well as several examples, came from their observations of their present and former firms.

## What Service Means to Clients: Eight General Factors

Clients have a difficult time evaluating the quality of professional services they receive because of four inherent characteristics of services. First, they are intangible; thus, they cannot be experienced in advance.

Second, services vary in quality because of individual differences. No two professionals deliver a service in precisely the same way. Clients differ, too. These differences make it very difficult for a firm to set, monitor, and enforce service delivery standards.

Third, services are produced and consumed simultaneously. Unlike a manufacturer, an accounting firm has no inventory. Fourth, few clients have the background to evaluate the technical aspects of a service. To evaluate service quality, clients must depend on their experiences during the service delivery process and their interactions with firm professionals. Eight general factors describe what service means to clients.

*Factor 1: Understanding Your Client's Business.* Accountants who truly understand a client's business look at the business on at least two levels. At one level, they understand how the financial statements are developed. Thus, they know how a client capitalizes equipment, how a client does bank reconciliations, how a client handles cash receipts. However, clients view their business as more than a technical report.

The client-oriented professional who understands the client's business knows its inner workings, how the parts fit together and interact, and comprehends its business cycles. For example, one CEO complained:

> Our accounting firm doesn't understand the cash-flow problems of our business, even though we have prepared a monthly statement and submitted it to our firm for 14 years. Most of our business takes place during two months, July and August. From May 1, the start of our fiscal year, until September 1, we really look great. Last September, after looking at the monthly statement, our tax partner called to say, "You're making a lot of money. You'll have to pay more money in." This tax partner still doesn't know we are a seasonal business—after 14 years.

Client-oriented firms focus continually on the question, "What is this company all about?" Client-oriented professionals know the client's product or service, and its markets. They make a point of spending time with managers who are not in financial areas. They use their understanding of the client's organization to help the client constructively, for example, "Your receivables are higher than we've ever seen them. What can we do to help you figure out what's going on?"

Once client-oriented professionals understand the client's business, they add the industry perspective, asking such questions as: How does this client resemble or differ from its peers? What characteristics do successful companies in this industry have? What are the prospects for the industry? What pressures does the industry face, and how do they affect our client?

To gain this perspective, you can participate in trade associations. Their meetings, conferences, training programs, and publications cover current issues facing the industry; in addition, over time you will learn the industry jargon. Frequently a trade association collects data that will allow you to compare your client with its peers on financial ratios and other performance measures.

Doing this analysis accomplishes three goals. First, you will learn more about your client and its relative performance. Second, when you discuss the analysis with your client, you communicate your desire to understand the business. Third, the analysis represents the basis for a business plan, which is a service your firm could offer clients.

Also beneficial is on-the-job training, which gives you experience with other clients in the industry and, possibly, with other professionals who are experienced in the industry. In this process, you are exposed to other types of operations and management approaches in the industry.

*Factor 2: Consistent Coordination of Service.* At first glance, the solo practitioner would appear to have an easy time coordinating services. Almost all client contact is with the practitioner, who, with a good secretary and a schedule, should keep everything straight. That works well until the practitioner is too successful—and overextended. In fact, one sign of overextension is the large number of requests for extensions filed with the Internal Revenue Service between April 1 and April 15 —in most cases for clients who really do not need extensions.

Once the solo practitioner realizes that his utilization rate is well over 100 percent and that he is a candidate for a heart attack, he could find a partner to share the existing workload and to ease service coordination. However, he will also have to share his income, which will be cut virtually in half.

A marketing orientation gives the solo practitioner another alternative, one that, in fact, is potentially more profitable. He could hire a partner who wants to develop business, but who needs a client base. By turning over a quarter of his practice (and a quarter of his income), the new partner gains a base, while the practitioner regains control over his practice. If the new partner successfully brings in new business, they have the foundation for further expansion.

In larger firms, coordination problems arise from having several professionals serving one client. A client-oriented firm organizes so that each client's service is coordinated by a management team of two or three people, whose responsibilities include bringing the right resources to serve the client. These service partners or managers make sure that the professionals performing work are briefed on the client's organization so that the client does not have to orient them. When a team member is reassigned or leaves the firm, the team is structured for transition, not serial replacement. Clients know what firm professionals will attend a meeting and find that these individuals are knowledgeable about the client organization. Client-oriented professionals do their homework.

One approach to ensuring service coordination is to establish a formal client service planning program that promotes consistent coordination. Among the firms developing such a program is Friedman, Eisenstein, Raemer & Schwartz, headquartered in Chicago. August Aquila, the firm's director of marketing, who meets with the partner in charge of the services to a particular client and other key professionals, summarizes his firm's approach:

> We review all aspects of the relationship, the services actually provided, additional services that could be provided, and referrals the client has made. Then, we develop a series of objectives and short-term action steps for each area. Our success indicators are client satisfaction and new business generated.

Formalizing the client service planning program is one way to communicate to your professionals and your clients that your firm places a high priority on service.

*Factor 3: Continuing Communication.* Communication is basic to understanding a client's business and to delivering coordinated service. One CEO summarized his need: "I want somebody to talk with, to relate to, on a continuing basis. The problem is to know who to talk to." In the client-oriented firm, the service management team has responsibility for consistent, clear, continuing communication between the firm and the client.

In this dialogue, the client's team feels free to describe its concerns and views openly and fully, while the service-team members bring their perspective, skills, and services. The service-management team then has the responsibility to incorporate the client's concerns into the service plan. Thus, if a client reports that a professional does not get along well with the client's staff, the service management team sees that the professional is not assigned to the client's work again. If a firm does not incorporate the client's legitimate requests into the actual service plan, that firm is not client-oriented.

To establish a successful firm-client dialogue, the firm's own internal communication systems must work. First, the service team must understand the firm's services and be able to communicate the benefits of these services to the client, even when a member of the service team cannot deliver the service. In larger firms which have a range of service lines, publications and training programs are two tools which can be used to educate service team management about the service lines.

In addition, communication channels must be open among the service team members. Consistent coordination of services does not necessarily indicate that communication among the firm's professionals is consistent and complete. Meetings of service-team members can be useful in keeping everyone informed, but informal means also should be used to keep the key team members up to date. Informal communications might include a memo about a telephone conversation with a client or a quick conversation over coffee with a partner or manager after a visit to the client.

When a practice is large enough to be departmentalized, team communication becomes a recurring problem. It is not unusual for the client of a departmentalized practice to use all its services—audit, tax, and consulting—and to deal with separate teams, each sending its own bill. You know you have a problem when a client says, "Doesn't anyone in your firm talk to each other?" With this question, that client has told you that he is evaluating one important aspect of your firm's service: communication.

**Factor 4: Responsiveness.** Client-oriented professionals understand their clients' priorities and deadlines, and strive to respond to them. The support systems in client-oriented firms are designed to help the professionals deliver quality services, and the professionals know how to use the systems efficiently. Thus, the service-management team directs engagement planning to ensure that staff time is used efficiently, client reports are developed quickly, and service levels are evaluated continually.

This is one of the easiest criteria for clients to evaluate because each client has deadlines or crises when it needs service. At such times, unresponsiveness is very apparent, as one CEO explains:

> Our year-end is June 30, and our big cash crunch always hits in late September and early October. Thus, we're in a tight time frame to get the audit done and to get approval for increased borrowing and lines of credit during August. Then we're in a position to borrow the money when we need it.
>
> Our accounting firm has never had the report ready on time. They finish the field work and give me a draft copy. Six weeks later, the report comes out of typing with no changes except for footnotes. In fact, we've never had a report, even a quarterly, that has taken fewer than six weeks for typing.

The CEO, then, concludes four times a year that his accounting firm is not responsive to his company's needs. If his firm does not compensate for this unresponsiveness, he is a candidate to change accounting firms.

This example also illustrates the usefulness of client feedback in improving a firm's operations. Perhaps there are bottlenecks in the firm's report processing group. Possibly junior people are drafting the report, with a manager reviewing the draft at the last minute. The point is that a firm's internal procedures and systems seem to be invisible to clients but they affect every client's perceptions of the firm.

***Factor 5: Staff Who Are Sensitive to Client Needs.*** When the service-management team does not understand the client's business, the results are inconsistent coordination of services and communication breakdown. In this situation, the junior staff is poorly trained in the area of client service and marketing skills. They are denied instruction directly, through role models on the job, and indirectly, through formal training programs. This is extremely detrimental to the firm because these younger professionals spend many hours in the client organization relating to the employees. In medium- and small-size companies, they often deal directly with the president or owner. As a result, they are frequently the most visible representatives of the accounting firm.

The effect on the client was described by one CEO: "We (clients) are being reminded periodically by this young, inexperienced person's presence that it seems as though we're not important." He described his relationship as "continually switching because of the high turnover in professionals assigned to our work. We don't have to change firms to switch."

The competence of staff professionals in performing technical work is not the issue. The fact that accounting firms must employ junior staff for certain tasks, just as junior staff must perform these tasks to gain experience, is accepted by clients. A client-oriented firm compensates for its staff's inexperience by having them review files and correspondence before beginning work so that they form a general picture of the client's business. The assignment of a new staff person might warrant a telephone call to the client, or even a visit from a partner or manager.

Formal training for young professionals is another means of helping them become sensitive to client needs. Among its advocates is Villanova University's William R. George:

> If we send professionals into a client organization and they disrupt operations and are insensitive to client needs, we are opening the door for that client to change accounting firms. Teaching younger staff marketing skills pays off because the contact person is essential to this relationship.[1]

***Factor 6: Sound Technical Skills.*** Many clients, unless they have an accounting background, find it difficult to evaluate an accounting firm on its technical skills. Only when the Internal

Revenue Service or some other third party calls does the client know that something may be wrong. Technical errors, particularly costly ones, can cause a client to change firms. A case in point illustrates the implicit trust clients have:

> In the statements audited by our former firm, there was a $1 million error in our net worth. For a $9 million company, that's a major error. On the basis of those statements, we spent over $3 million in expansion, buying new property and equipment. We had a false sense of security. Reality hit when we realized that we had no money and were on the brink of bankruptcy. In granting a loan to bail us out, the bank forced us to change accounting firms.

Client-oriented firms not only build in procedures to ensure that client reports are correct, but they also develop the skills to convert the report information into a benefit for the client (e.g., by forecasting a problem or by giving a "quick and dirty" answer to a tax problem). The client then has the means to evaluate technical service when he verifies that the problem occurred, was avoided, or was solved.

*Factor 7: Value for Fees Paid.* Many professionals believe that the primary service issue to clients is price. That is true under one set of conditions: The client does not perceive that it is receiving special attention, that the professionals understand the client's business, and that the firm brings any special experience to the engagement. The only event initiated is the start of the audit. In this scenario, firms look alike, so price is paramount.

One CEO defines *value* with this example: "I used to be able to telephone our tax partner and get an answer to a question in three minutes. I don't care if he costs $1,000 an hour. That's value. Now our tax advice isn't as valuable. I miss it so much. I think a lot about making a change because of it." Client-oriented professionals find out how a client defines *value*, and they strive to deliver service consistent with that definition. Because they understand the client's business, they can initiate discussions with the client about problems and opportunities, and they help to identify alternative solutions that assist the client in achieving its goals.

For clients concerned with value, price may also represent a socially acceptable explanation for changing accounting firms. In most cases, a close personal relationship develops between a client and one or more of the firm's professionals. In delivering service, the professional becomes part of the service. When the professional is integral to the client's service experience, it is difficult for the client to tell the professional that the firm's service is not up to par because he does not want to lose the personal relationship and does not want to get his friend in trouble. Managing partners do not look favorably on partners and managers whose clients become unhappy with the firm's service and leave.

When the professional was apprised of the client's dissatisfaction, she probably would react with promises to improve the level of service and undoubtedly would try to deliver. She would be successful if the service delivery systems in the firm were ready to support and sustain change. However, from the client's perspective, these promises may only mean a delay of the inevitable change. In addition, by avoiding the service discussion, the client would remain on good terms with the firm's professionals. Thus, price becomes the apparent reason for the change, and the professionals falsely perceive that they have more evidence for the importance of price in the decision to change firms.

***Factor 8: Making the Client Feel Valued.*** "I want an accounting firm that treats me like a customer," stated one CEO, who knows something about how customers like to be treated; his repeat business from first-year customers is 70 percent. A second *Inc.* 500 CEO, concurs: "It's human nature to believe that once you pay someone for a service, he owes you something. My sense is that the first thing an accounting firm owes its clients is to make us feel important." He continues:

> I really don't know how we would go about changing firms. I have come to believe that a lot of what we would hear at the beginning

just isn't so. I don't know how well we can anticipate what it's really going to be like. How do you determine that you'll be a valued client?

Some of the experiences that did not make them feel valued were described in earlier sections. Your firm has many opportunities to say, "You are a valued client." They range from the simple, for example, the prompt return of a telephone call and the support of a client's charity, to the more elaborate, such as client profiles in your newsletters and invitations to business and social events sponsored by your firm.

Your firm's clients are continually evaluating your firm—its services, delivery systems, and professionals. This evaluation process, which may be quite informal, covers the eight general criteria just discussed. To clients, service means: (1) understanding their business; (2) consistent coordination of service; (3) communication; (4) responsiveness; (5) staff who are sensitive to clients' needs; (6) sound technical skills; (7) value for the fees paid; and (8) feeling valued by the firm. Professionals in the client-oriented firm recognize that, with the exception of the technical skills criterion, all the criteria concern the client's interaction with firm professionals and the ways service is delivered to clients.

## How Clients Select an Accounting Firm: Seven Criteria

When a financial vice president or a business owner evaluates an accounting firm which is a candidate to provide services, he does not have the experience with the candidate firm to judge whether its services will satisfy his needs. While a current client has good experiential evidence of a firm's service quality, the potential client must look for evidence that gives promise of good service. The potential client formulates selection criteria indicating or implying the firm's credibility.

In this section, we describe the seven selection factors that financial executives and business owners believe are important. These factors derive from our analysis of seven studies of the auditor selection process.[2] The factors, reflecting the consistency of response across studies, provide a framework for understanding the process. The relative importance of the factors depends on the individual prospective client. The following section concerns a subgroup of potential clients—clients that are changing accounting firms. They have an experience base that may make certain factors more important than others, and the client-oriented firm must determine their concerns.

*Image/Reputation.* An accounting firm's reputation is the most important selection factor cited by executives. Reputation or image may seem difficult to gauge because business people gain frequent impressions of accounting firms from a large number of sources with varying reliability. Yet, there are specific criteria prospective clients cite as useful indicators of image.

Client recommendations

Third-party recommendations (e.g., lawyers)

Knowledge of the partners in the firm

A firm's current client list

The client-centered firm manages its reputation. First, the firm conducts research to obtain objective feedback about its reputation with clients and the business community. In effect, you will learn if your audiences, or markets, perceive your firm in the same way you and your partners do. Major differences point to problems you can fix. For example, your partners may believe the firm is well known to bankers, who frequently refer business. Your research may show that this perception is correct. If so, you are on target.

If the perception is incorrect and if you want to develop this referral source, you can formulate a plan to make your firm known to bankers. The research results, then, become the basis for directing the firm's image program, as well as the benchmark against which the results of the image-building program are compared to measure the program's success.

***Quality of the Professionals.*** The firm's professionals to be assigned to the client's work represent another important concern to prospective clients. Clients are interested in:

1. the rapport between the firm's professionals and the client's management team
2. the experience and depth of the audit personnel assigned
3. the overall quality of the staff

Professionals in client-oriented firms seek opportunities to get together with people in the potential client's organization, so that they can begin to understand the business, its goals, and its needs. They arrange interviews and site surveys with the potential client's managers early in the proposal process. The opportunity to learn more about the client's organization, plans, and opportunities, as well as to exchange ideas, gives both sides valuable information about the prospects for the relationship.

Client-oriented professionals explain why their firm's team members were selected, what special competencies they have and the relationship of these competencies to the prospective client's needs, and what particular benefits the client can expect from working with these professionals. They emphasize these points in meetings and in written materials, particularly in proposals.

***Accessibility of the Professionals.*** Prospective clients want to know that the accounting firm's professionals, particularly the top people, are available and accessible. This factor is especially important to small business clients. Obviously, accessibility is difficult to evaluate prior to service. Client-centered professionals determine if the client needs a particular specialty (e.g., tax or mergers and acquisitions). If so, the specialist is assigned to the service team. Similarly, if the prospective client needs the perspective of an industry specialist, this professional becomes an important team member.

One indicator of accessibility potential clients use frequently is the location of offices, that is, the proximity of the firm's offices to the company's business locations—both national and international. Client-oriented firms determine if this is a concern to the potential client and find a solution that satisfies that concern. The solution might be a commitment to hold twice-monthly meetings at the client's office. Another approach might be to open a satellite office in the community.

*Quality of Service.* As we discussed earlier, it is very difficult to evaluate service before experiencing it. One cannot tell in advance whether an accounting firm will meet deadlines or not. Interoffice work consistency cannot be determined either. The client-centered firm knows what elements of its service delivery process are valued by its clients because the firm has asked its clients about them. As a result, the firm has revised or refined the internal systems supporting those elements clients value.

Its professionals can describe to potential clients specific examples of service quality. For example, when a potential client tells a client-centered professional that his borrowing needs come two months after year-end, the professional can reply that 80 percent of the reports of comparable scope are delivered to the client in six to seven weeks after year-end. Facts count with prospective clients.

If interoffice work consistency is a concern, the firm's approach to setting standards in this area should be described, and clients who have operations in multiple locations should be used as references. Open communication is another example of a prospective client's concern. Develop a service planning process that involves the client in planning meetings so that he can communicate with the team in order that both points of view are understood.

*Breadth and Depth of Services.* Prospective clients want to know that the services they need will be available and will be tailored to their industry. They look for a full range of general services (e.g., management consulting, employee benefits consulting) and services geared to clients having special needs (e.g., small business, government regulatory experience).

An executive or a business owner wants to know that the firm selected has professionals who understand not only the industry, but also the ways to help a client succeed in that industry. The client-centered firm establishes its credibility with a professional who understands and speaks the industry jargon and who can relate client experiences relevant to the prospective client.

Professionals in the client-oriented firm understand that many potential clients are not finance specialists and, therefore, have a limited understanding of a firm's services. The client-oriented firm recognizes the need to educate the potential client about the firm's services and to demonstrate how the services satisfy the prospect's needs.

There are several basic ways to educate potential clients about your firm's services. First, the firm's marketing brochure addresses prospective clients' needs and relates the firm's services toward meeting those needs. The brochure, then, is as much, if not more, about "you" (the prospective client) as it is about "us" (the accounting firm). Second, the firm's professionals usually have a series of meetings with a prospective client; they include site visits, interviews, and presentations. The professionals should take advantage of each meeting to identify services needed and to describe relevant services. Third, these discussions can be reinforced in written communications, including follow-up letters and proposals.

*Technical Competence.* If evaluating an accounting firm on its technical competence is difficult for clients, it is even harder for prospective clients. After all, technically knowledgeable executives need the benefit of experience to evaluate a firm in this area. Yet technical excellence is a concern.

The client-oriented firm addresses this concern by the involvement of professionals in trade and professional associations and by building this involvement into the firm's image campaign. For example, if a partner serves on a technical committee of the state society or a trade association, that involvement should be publicized in the business press and in firm publications. When that partner's résumé is prepared for a proposal, his committee work should be detailed.

The firm also addresses the prospective client's specific technical concerns. For example, when meeting with a prospective client, professionals can ask about current technical questions and offer alternate solutions to give the prospective client the firm's perspective.

*Fees.* In many accounting firms, the conventional wisdom is that price is the potential client's most important factor in selecting an accounting firm. Although the business executives participating in all seven studies cited fees as important in the selection process, this factor did not rank first or second in importance in any study. Many professionals, surprised at this finding, would respond that, in their day-to-day experience, prospective clients are extremely concerned about price. We would agree, with one modification: Prospective clients are very concerned about price in relation to value.

If the prospective client does not understand how a firm's services will benefit his organization, price is a primary consideration. In fact, in selecting among several technically oriented firms, it may be the only factor differentiating one firm from another. The client-oriented firm provides the evidence for the potential client to conclude that the firm can help the client organization achieve its goals.

## Why Companies Change Accounting Firms

Every year hundreds of organizations change accounting firms at some expense to their staffs in terms of time and disruption to work schedules. What prompts an executive—usually the chief financial officer or the president—to consider change? In order of importance, the eight reasons cited most frequently are as follows.

Fees too high
Deteriorating quality of service in:

Audit
Management consulting
Tax
Difficulties in working with some of the firm's professionals
Need for additional services
Audit scope too large
Need for a better-known accounting firm
Difference of opinion on accounting issues
Staff turnover/reassignment[3]

Most changes, it should be noted, have multiple causes, as indicated by the fact that many executives surveyed gave several responses. The decision to change firms is complex, but one point is clear: Price is important when clients do not perceive value. The client-centered firm finds out why clients leave (from the client's perspective) and uses this information to improve its service quality and service delivery systems.

Does the executive who has had a negative experience have a different set of priorities in selecting a new firm? One *Inc.* 500 CEO, committed to changing firms, had been speaking with professionals from several firms. He summarized the process he was going through:

> First, my internal accounting staff and I must like the individual selling us. We've narrowed the field down to three firms, and we'll spend the next few months interviewing them. All the firms we've talked to say the same thing, word for word—how they can cut the bill, how they can streamline the audit. We did find one firm that gave us some industry statistics that helped us a lot. The firm we choose will have specific ideas about how the company can develop.

For this CEO, price will be a criterion in selecting a new firm:

> Our product is more expensive than our competitors', and yet we have 70 percent market share. We use a very expensive law firm that gives us good service, and we've never had even a minor argu-

ment about a bill. We don't dispute price. On the accounting side, I think our present firm sends me a bill whenever they have nothing to do. Our costs have gone up, but we aren't getting the service we want.

The accounting firms are notorious for buying business the first year, so we have thought about changing firms every year because each firm looks at last year's bill and says, "Oh, we can do this for 30 percent less." If we could get the service we want, we wouldn't mind paying the price. However, we're not very optimistic about finding a firm that will give us the service we want, so price will be important.

Clients changing accounting firms are influenced by their experience with a previous firm and, in fact, may draw conclusions about all accounting firms from that experience.

When a professional in a client-centered firm discusses service with a prospective client who is changing firms, the professional tries to understand the effect of the client's experience on his expectations of the professional's firm. Also, the professional tries to identify the service lapses upon which the client-centered firm may be able to capitalize if it can demonstrate those capabilities.

## ☐ GAIN A COMPETITIVE EDGE

Because an accounting firm's client is involved in the service process at several levels, the client has information and insights about both its organization and its accounting firm that are valuable to the accounting firm. If your firm is to have a competitive edge, you must systematically capture this information from current, former, and future clients.

### Six Benefits of Client-Centered Management

A client-centered firm's investment in service quality pays off in at least six areas. Undoubtedly, professionals in your firm will be able to add others.

*Satisfied Clients Buy Additional Services.* First, every client who values the firm's services is a candidate for other current or planned services that meet his needs. These additional services, when delivered well, not only add to the firm's revenues, but also further cement the firm-client relationship.

*Satisfied Clients Refer Business.* Every client who values the services he receives is a source of new clients. The client-centered firm can ask that client to refer other business executives to the firm for services, and a satisfied client will do so. That client also represents a recommendation to prospective clients who have similar business needs. Thus, a satisfied client helps the firm generate new business.

*Satisfied Clients Enhance the Firm's Reputation.* A satisfied client describes the firm's services positively to his banker and his lawyer, who represent referral sources to the firm. He also speaks well of the firm to other members of the business community (e.g., the press), thus enhancing the firm's reputation.

*Satisfied Clients Are Profitable.* Operationally, it is much better to serve one client continually than to have that client leave and, in effect, necessitate replacement. The firm should be able to maintain a higher profit level with an existing client as compared with a new client due to the expense of acquiring and developing new business. If that client leaves, the firm incurs high start-up costs with the replacement client in both service delivery and relationship building. Old money is better than new in this scenario.

*Satisfied Clients Want a Growth-Oriented Firm.* The satisfied client wants the client-centered firm to grow in tandem with it. Client needs point to new services which the firm can develop and deliver to existing clients and which make the client-centered firm attractive to potential clients.

*Satisfied Clients Help Professionals Develop.* A satisfied client provides growth experiences for the client-centered firm's professionals. They understand that client's business, and, in the process of helping the client grow, they have learned a great deal, formed constructive business and personal relationships, and had fun.

***Dissatisfaction Hurts Your Firm and Its Professionals.*** These benefits make obvious the results of dissatisfaction: poor recommendations to potential new clients and to referral sources, reduced opportunities for additional services, lost clients, frustrated professionals. Client dissatisfaction damages a firm's reputation. Client satisfaction enhances it.

The perceptions of your firm's clients are measurable. You must determine whether your firm wants to understand them or not. Choosing not to obtain this data means that your firm will be in a reactive position in the competitive times ahead. Having hard data about your clients' needs and satisfactions empowers you (1) to manage your firm more effectively, and (2) to manage your client relationships.

## How to Use Client Feedback to Manage Your Firm

Client satisfaction correlates with service quality. and, thus, the better the service, the higher the client's satisfaction. Service quality is composed of two interdependent dimensions: technical quality and functional quality.[4] In most accounting firms, the technical quality dimension is high. Firms have long used such techniques as second-partner review to ensure that technical standards are established and maintained.

Functional quality (i.e., how the service is delivered to the client) focuses on the firm's professionals—their accessibility, attitudes, appearance, behaviors, interpersonal skills, and relationships with other professionals. This dimension underlies the client's experiences with the firm, which are the primary basis for the client's perceptions of a firm's quality. In accounting firms, less emphasis has been placed on service delivery than on technical quality, in large part because service delivery is difficult for firms to define and control. Yet its importance cannot be denied.

The client-centered firm, using research support, surveys its clients to identify specific service strengths and weaknesses. The firm directs these findings to the appropriate department in the firm for action. Let's examine how client feedback is useful to specific functions.

*Service Delivery Systems.* The client-centered firm is interested in its clients' specific experiences with the firm's service delivery systems, including the timeliness of report delivery, the coordination of service, the client's familiarity with the services offered by the firm, the accuracy of bills, the importance of price. Troublesome areas get fixed; problems do not recur. The focus is on improving service, *not* on punishing professionals for untimely or unresponsive service in the past. In fact, a firm's professionals and support personnel have many ideas about ways to improve service. The client-centered firm gives them responsibility for identifying and implementing service quality programs.

*Human Resources.* Human resources staff can use feedback to improve recruiting, training, and reward systems. The attitudinal traits important to functional quality translate into criteria for recruiting professionals who can build strong client relationships. The sensitivity clients want in their professionals enters into training requirements for communication and listening skills, industry and other types of specialization, and an understanding of the firm's services in total. The client-centered firm rewards and promotes professionals who understand the client frame of reference. Thus, evaluation criteria for all professionals, even the technical gurus, stress quality in service delivery.

*Marketing.* In the marketing area, there are several obvious uses of client feedback. New services can be developed on the basis of data-driven client needs. The client-centered firm has a good understanding of its reputation because it has systematically obtained the perceptions of its most important constituency—its clients. The messages the client-centered firm communicates to its public have a basis in reality; the messages are simple, direct, and credible. Thus, the firm's promotional campaigns—whether public relations, advertising, or other tools—have consistency and focus.

*Internal Marketing.* The effect of client perceptions on the client-centered firm's internal marketing program (comprised of the joint efforts of the marketing, human resources, and technical departments) is not as obvious as its direct promotional campaigns. The client-centered firm recognizes that its professionals and support staff:

> "Can be influenced most effectively and hence motivated to customer consciousness, market orientation, and salesmindedness . . . by using marketing-like activities internally."[5]

In the client-centered firm, management recognizes that partners and staff do not want to lose clients, and provides the support to help them serve clients well.

A shift toward a client-centered orientation requires a change in the focus of many functions your firm has today. While this process involves time (which is money), it does not necessitate large direct expenditures. What drives the shift in orientation is the commitment of the firm's management group.

## How to Keep Clients Happy: Four Critical Points

Understanding clients' perceptions of your firm's service quality allows you to manage your client relationships. A client's perceptions of service quality actually begin to take shape during the selection process when your firm's professionals describe its qualifications and make promises about the service level and the benefits the client will gain. The potential client builds a set of expectations about the service your firm will deliver.

*The Sale.* The sale is an especially critical point for both the client and the professional.[6] Then, the client is anticipating the attention he will receive as your firm's client. His mood is up. He starts to evaluate the consistency between his expectations and the service received. When the two are in sync, he is pleased. When your professionals deliver more than the client expected, he is even more pleased. The danger point arises when the client expects more than your professionals deliver.

When the professionals gain a new client, they "peak" because of the concentrated proposal effort they made. Success was gaining a new client. Now they have other things to catch up on. When they shift their attention, they disappoint the client by not giving him the service he expects.

With planning, this disappointment can be avoided. For example, a member of the service management team can schedule a meeting with the appropriate client representatives as soon as possible. In one firm, the partner in charge of the practice invites the new client's decision makers to a reception or luncheon. By recognizing this critical point, you can take action to influence client perceptions.

**Project Completion.** Another critical time is the completion of any special work you may do—a consulting project, perhaps. The client may not understand the benefits her organization has obtained as a result of the project. Your role is to communicate these benefits to the appropriate people in the client organization, including the decision makers if they were not the buyers of the project. During this process, you can obtain useful feedback about the client's perceptions of service delivery and quality.

**Planning.** The planning phase of any work offers opportunity to manage client perceptions because you can educate the client about the process you will follow and the results the client can expect to see at various points. Frequently, clients do not understand why a procedure takes so long or why it is even needed. If you can anticipate and deal with some of these questions during the planning phase, you effectively reduce the likelihood of client dissatisfaction later in the engagement.

*No Activity.* A fourth critical time is that period when your firm is doing no work for a client. You then must initiate proposals to help the client, invite him to events he considers worthwhile, or find another way for him to conclude, "This firm is interested in my organization. Their professionals initiate things. They have good ideas."

There are other critical times you can identify from your clients' experiences, their business cycles, and your own observations. Managing client perceptions involves obtaining this information systematically and using it to build constructive working relationships with your clients.

## ☐ SERVICE ORIENTATION—PHILOSOPHY

Creating and keeping a client—Peter Drucker's definition of marketing is especially meaningful to professional service organizations, which are founded on solid, long-term client relationships. Client service is the core of a firm, its philosophy.

Client-oriented firms have a continuing dialogue with clients in which the firm learns from its clients and uses their insights to improve service. Effective client service drives a firm's image, attracts creative professionals who enjoy solving clients' problems, and yields loyal, long-term clients. Firms which serve clients well have the foundation to market well, to grow and prosper.

## ☐ NOTES

1. See also Richard M. Murray and William R. George, "Managing CPA Personnel—A Marketing Perspective," *CPA Journal* (July 1979): 17–22.
2. The Conference Board, *Corporations and Their Outside Auditors* (New York: The Conference Board, Inc., 1972). The sample comprised 490 senior financial executives; over 60 percent were associated with companies having sales of $100 million or more. Over 90 percent of the companies were audited by Big Eight firms. The survey questionnaire consisted of open-ended questions. The volunteered responses yielded two criteria as most important: "reputation" and "expertise in auditing."

William R. George and Paul J. Solomon, "Marketing Strategies for Improving Practice Development," *The Journal of Accountancy* (February 1980): 79–82. The sample consisted of 286 business executives in four cities: Cincinnati, Houston, Richmond, and Seattle. Representing a response rate of 48.5 percent, the sample crossed industries and had sales ranging from under $5 million to over $100 million. The responses to a questionnaire yielded the following factors as most influential: location of CPA firm's offices, client recommendations, third-party recommendations, industry specialization, and breadth of services offered.

Bradford W. Ketchum, Jr., "You and Your Accountants; How to Evaluate the Relationship between You and Your Company's Most Important Adviser," *Inc.* (March 1982): 81–90. The survey queried 5,000 small business executives, 20.4 percent of whom responded. Among the respondents, privately held corporations predominated (84 percent), with average annual sales of $5.1 million. The two most important factors in selecting an accounting firm were "personal contact" and "reputation."

Management Analysis Center, Inc., "On Switching (Rotating?) Audit Firms," *Directors and Boards* (Spring 1977): 51–59. The chief financial officers or the chief executive officers of 293 publicly held companies that had changed accounting firms from 1970 to 1976 were surveyed via a mailed questionnaire. They represented 22 percent of the total sample. Of the 293 companies, 76 percent reported sales of less than $50 million. The most important selection criteria they cited were the firm's reputation and the accessibility of the firm's top people.

Reichman Research, Inc., and Deloitte Haskins & Sells, *An Opinion Survey of the Public Accounting Profession* (New York: Reichman Research, Inc., 1978). The sample consisted of 464 corporate financial officers, who agreed to be interviewed. The two characteristics that emerged as most important in "selecting/evaluating" an accounting firm were "technical competence" and "overall reputation."

Tyzoon T. Tyebjee and Albert V. Bruno, "Developing the Marketing Concept in Public Accounting Firms," *Journal of the Academy of Marketing Science* (Spring 1982): 165–188. Participating in the survey were 112 of the 140 privately held, high-technology firms located in the San Francisco Bay Area and having 15 to 150 employees. Their auditors were evenly divided between national and local firms. The chief executive officer or the chief financial officer of each company was interviewed by telephone. The three most important criteria identified were rapport, attention from audit and tax partners, and timely service.

The *Wall Street Journal, The Balance Sheet: Top Executives Speak Out about CPA Firms* (New York: Dow Jones & Co., Inc., 1978). The sample consisted of half the 1,000 *Fortune* industrials and the 300 companies on the Fortune "Top 50" lists, as well as a random sample of 250 companies with sales in the $50 million to $100 million range. The overall response rate was 61.8 percent. A CPA firm's reputation was the factor considered most important in selecting a firm.

3. See note 2: The Conference Board, 1972; Management Analysis Center, 1977; and Reichman Research and Deloitte Haskins & Sells, 1978.

4. See Christian Grönroos, *Strategic Management and Marketing in the Service Sector* (Cambridge, Mass.: Marketing Science Institute, 1983), 20–27.

5. Grönroos, p. 77.

6. See Theodore Levitt, *The Marketing Imagination* (New York: The Free Press, 1983), 117–18.

# 2

## MARKETING STRATEGIES THAT WORK

What are successful marketing programs? They are the configuration of activities a firm engages in to strengthen client relationships and attract new clients. Whether you are a sole proprietor or a large multioffice firm, you will want to make the right decisions in setting up your marketing program so that you achieve these results. You will need to answer such questions as:

Where should you begin?
Who should be involved?
How much should be budgeted?
What kind of results can you expect?
When can you expect the results?

To arrive at the answers that are right for you and your partners, you will need to make some hard decisions. Fortunately, there is a process to guide you through these key decisions: the strategic market planning process. The elements involved in formulating and implementing a strategic marketing plan for your firm can help focus your marketing efforts on the activities that will best meet your firm's needs. That is the subject of this chapter. Specifically, we will answer the question: *How can your firm develop effective marketing strategies?* This question focuses on:

1. Meeting the needs of your clients
2. Using the discipline of marketing effectively
3. Developing your firm's professionals
4. Obtaining measurable results

## □ WHAT IS THE STRATEGIC MARKETING PROCESS?

Whether you are a sole proprietorship or a large complex firm with multiple sites and services, the strategic marketing process involves two basic components. First, a plan must be developed for every service or industry type your firm offers—from simple tax return preparation to the complex management advisory services. The second component requires the integration of all these service or industry plans into a firm-wide strategic marketing plan. This integration process, which most firms do not do, is the key ingredient to increase your firm's marketing effectiveness and will ensure that you use your resources effectively and efficiently.

### How to Develop a Plan

Developing a plan for each service or industry/specialty group is the initial step in strategic marketing. As we shall see, a plan does not need to be lengthy, but it must be well conceived and presented clearly. The first plan you develop will serve as a model as your firm expands into new services or client industries. You also can use your initial plan as a guide in developing service plans for your current services. If your firm has several existing services or industry/specialty groups, the optimal time to have them develop plans is during your firm's business planning cycle.

To develop a service plan, you must proceed through eight phases.

1. Identify client or market needs.
2. Analyze the competition.
3. Analyze the firm's capabilities\to meet the needs.
4. Define the service offered.
5. Delegate responsibility for the service.
6. Design external communications.
7. Develop internal communications.
8. Evaluate and control the plan.

The process of developing a service plan is progressive; that is, you should not progress to the next phase in the process unless the current phase is understood. Table 2-1 lists the eight phases of your firm's service plan, identifies the best sources of information, and specifies the types of questions that you must answer at each phase. For clarity, the table includes an example of a specific service—personal financial planning—with the appropriate action plan required to answer the questions posed. Later, we will present a sample service plan for personal financial planning.

***Phase 1: Identify Client or Market Needs.*** To be client centered, your firm must formulate service plans based on the needs of your clients or prospects. This information can only be obtained from clients, referral sources, or prospects. The following questions must be answered.

Who needs the service?
What services are they currently using?
Are they satisfied with these services?
What type of services do they perceive they need?
What additional services are desired?
What is the firm's ability to render new services?

To effectively answer these questions, you must gather information systematically. Many accounting professionals feel con-

**TABLE 2–1. SERVICE PLAN PROCESS**

| Phase | Sources of Information | General Information Required | Specific Example: Personal Financial Planning (PFP) | |
| --- | --- | --- | --- | --- |
| | | | Specific Information Required | Action Plan |
| Identify needs | Clients, referral sources, prospects | What services are they currently using? Are they satisfied with current services? What additional services are desired? What is the firm's ability to render the new service? Why should your firm offer the new service? | What are the demographics of clients in need of PFP? Who should be targeted for PFP? What are their PFP needs? How can PFP benefit clients? What is the perception of PFP? How can a CPA firm offer better PFP services than non-CPAs? | Perform an informal survey of clients, referral sources Conduct a formal market survey |
| Analyze the competition | Business community (advertising in media, discussion with referral sources, etc.) | Who is your competition? Is the competition offering the same or a similar service? | Who is offering PFP services? What are other CPA firms doing in this area? Is the competition approaching our clients? Are Certified Financial Planners (CFP) operating in this area? What are the going fees for this service? | Evaluate business journals Call network of associates Evaluate competition's services Obtain and analyze competition's literature Ask clients about PFP from other sources |
| Identify firm capabilities | Partners, managers, accounting/consulting staff | What services does the firm render? Where does the new service fit with the firm? | Does the service fit into the tax department? What services are already available? What services need to be added? | Examine staff capabilities Obtain CFP information List all tax-related services Examine PFP report |

| | | | | |
|---|---|---|---|---|
| Define service | Partners | What staff training is required?<br>What procedures need to be developed?<br>What are the service's features or benefits?<br>Who will be in charge of the new service?<br>What policies have to be modified or developed?<br>What will be the fee for this service?<br>What will be the budget for marketing the new service? | What professional will be the PFP coordinator?<br>What additional training is needed for the PFP coordinator?<br>What technical procedures and controls need to be developed?<br>Will the PFP service be customized or standard?<br>Will the PFP fees be based on hourly or unit rate?<br>Who will be responsible for the PFP service?<br>What internal systems need modification to support PFP?<br>How is the client interaction structured (e.g., format reports, meetings, printed materials)?<br>What will be the budget for introducing and supporting PFP service? | Perform cost analysis<br>Set PFP fee structure<br>Delegate responsibility<br>Set formal procedures and control policies<br>Develop client materials/reports<br>Develop marketing budget<br>Assign PFP service coordinator |
| Coordinate new service | Assigned accounting professional and marketing professional | What is the marketing plan?<br>What staff will provide the service?<br>What staff will assist in selling the service?<br>What additional staff training is required?<br>Are there any marketing materials that could aid staff in selling? | What is the specific PFP marketing plan?<br>What staff will provide PFP?<br>What staff will assist in selling PFP?<br>What additional staff training is required?<br>What materials are required to sell PFP? | Analyze and identify marketing strategies<br>Select staff for technical training<br>Plan internal communications program<br>Analyze staff and client needs for commonality |

**TABLE 2–1.** (Continued)

| | | | Specific Example: Personal Financial Planning (PFP) | |
| --- | --- | --- | --- | --- |
| Phase | Sources of Information | General Information Required | Specific Information Required | Action Plan |
| Develop market plan | Assigned accounting professional and marketing professional | What is the best mix of marketing strategies? What marketing tools are required? What are the communication/advertising plans? What internal systems are necessary to support marketing efforts? | How do clients, prospects and referral sources obtain PFP information/education? What is the PFP message most pertinent to targeted audiences? When would be the most efficient and effective time to reach the targeted market? Why is it important to use a CPA for PFP? What print media do targeted clients read? Would seminars contribute to interest in PFP? What printed materials are necessary for direct mailing, follow-up pieces, and so on? Should self-sustaining seminar materials be developed to educate prospects/clients? What advertising should be used? What public relations tools can be used? | Select marketing message Define marketing program Develop one-year marketing plan Prepare supplemental materials Develop firm educational program Set program timetable Select appropriate advertising, public relations, etc. Incorporate into client service planning. |

| Develop internal communication plan | Assigned accounting professional and marketing professional | How do we communicate new service to staff? How do we enhance staff's understanding of the new service? How do we update staff on new service developments? How do we help staff sell new service? | Can existing internal materials include PFP aspect? Can PFP be incorporated into proposals for other services? Can PFP be incorporated into industry-related information? What staff members should be aware of PFP? Should nonaccounting staff be advised as to PFP service availability? If yes, how? Can materials be developed to train/educate staff as well as clients on PFP? | Assign responsibilities to professionals Develop support materials Develop internal communications plan Inform staff of public relations and advertising programs |
|---|---|---|---|---|
| Evaluate and control plan | Assigned accounting professional and marketing professional | How do we track results of program? How is the system to be controlled? When should results be expected? How will staff be evaluated? Who is responsible for staff evaluation? When will client feedback/evaluation be obtained? | Have we sold any PFP business? How much? To whom? What procedures should staff follow after locating a tentative client? What do clients like about PFP? Dislike? | Design or modify new business reporting system Develop staff training program Design and implement communications network Conduct client research regarding satisfaction with PFP |

fident that they know their clients' answers to these questions. However, research has shown that accountants do not have the same opinion or perspective as their clients.[1] Also, when accountants ask their clients for information, it may be difficult to get honest, unbiased answers from the clients without fear of damaging the relationship. Thus, accountants do not ask, and clients do not volunteer information.

In order to make sound decisions, your firm will have to evaluate current client problems and potential opportunities. You have a number of alternatives available. Many firms already have information in their files that can be reorganized to reveal a wealth of knowledge about client needs.

Surveys, both formal and informal, are also important sources of information. Formal surveys—by mail or telephone, as well as in personal interviews and focus groups—require development and coordination by marketing professionals or researchers. Many firms have successfully worked with area colleges or universities to perform surveys. This collaboration has helped many firms solve the time and expense constraints.

Informal surveys may include a simple questionnaire used by your accounting professionals when providing service to clients. In any case, it is important to recognize the value of obtaining unbiased data to determine whether a service represents a growth opportunity. Such data can lead to improved or refined services, identification of new services, and a better understanding of how your clients perceive your services.

The type of research you conduct is dependent on the objectives of your service plan. In our personal financial planning example in Table 2-1, the questions were answered through a combination of a formal market survey and an informal client questionnaire. The major objective in the surveys was to determine if personal financial planning represents a growth opportunity for the firm. With the assistance of a marketing department at a local university's business school, a formal market survey was undertaken to determine the growth potential in the firm's current market. This survey examined a broad range of client-accountant relationships and services, including personal financial planning. Simultaneously, an informal client survey based on a simple questionnaire was conducted by accounting professionals to determine the interest of individual and corporate clients in personal financial planning services.

Combining an informal client survey (which determines current needs and perceptions) with the formal market survey (which determines the service's growth potential) provides a firm with the information needed to make client-oriented decisions. If the results show that clients perceive a need for the service and if the service offers an opportunity for growth, the next phase is to analyze the competition to determine how unique this service is in your market.

***Phase 2: Analyze the Competition.*** When developing a service plan, you must assess your competitors to determine the uniqueness of the service. The following questions must be answered.

Who is your competition?

Is the competition offering the same or a similar service?

How are they marketing the service?

What are they charging for this service?

Answers to these questions should help you determine the feasibility of offering, or continuing to offer, the service.

Competitive intelligence can be easily obtained. Simply review the business publications offered in your market, and collect all related articles or advertising on the particular or similar service. Your clients and referral sources also have valuable information about competitive activities. Check with professional and trade organizations to identify firms which specialize in the service. When you gain a new client who obtained proposals from several firms, ask the client to let you review the other firms' proposals.

The personal financial planning example in Table 2-1 illustrates the specific questions that should be addressed in your particular business environment. The results of your competitive analysis will help you reassess your firm's position in the market. Look for the one or two differentiating elements that separate your firm from the competition, and focus your marketing program on this uniqueness.

Once you have gathered and evaluated information about the competition and matched these results with the information on client or market needs, you next must examine the firm's internal structure to determine the feasibility of offering the service.

***Phase 3: Identify Firm Capabilities.*** The third phase in the service plan is to identify firm capabilities: Can your firm offer the service that clients need and want? In a technically oriented firm, the wrong step often comes first: A capability is identified before a client's need is established. Thus, some services are successful, while others fail for no apparent reason. As we discussed earlier, the growth of your firm depends on your firm being client centered. First, identify the client need, and then determine how your firm can supply the service to satisfy the need.

As a result of the surveys and the information gathered in the first phase of the service plan, a number of client needs have been identified. Now you must look at the firm's capabilities, in terms of both personnel and operations, and match the capabilities and interests with the needs. The following questions need to be discussed.

What services does the firm currently render?

Where does the new service fit within the firm?

What staff training is required?

What procedures need to be developed?

In the personal financial planning example in Table 2-1, specific questions are posed that must be answered satisfactorily if the service is to be institutionalized.

Once a match in personnel ability has been found, the firm must also examine whether it can provide the service. Will it be necessary to modify present procedures and system controls? How can the firm structure its operations to support the new service? An additional service can impose operational stress on the firm and, therefore, create internal problems. Unless these questions are addressed and resolved in advance, the service may meet resistance from both professional staff and potential clients whose expectations are not met because internal systems are inadequate. If a new service is offered and the appropriate systems are in place to support it, the service will have a better chance of success.

*Phase 4: Define the Service.* The service plan also requires that you define the new service. This phase involves giving the service some tangible qualities or features, delegating responsibility for the service, and defining a budget for its introduction and support.

What are the benefits of the service? From the surveys performed in the first phase of the service plan, a number of benefits should have been identified. Listing these benefits will give the service tangibility because clients will be able to relate to them. For instance, in our example of personal financial planning, one obvious short-term benefit would be tax savings. By listing the benefits and giving the service tangibility, your firm will be able to determine whether it is a realistic service to offer.

Another area to define is responsibility for the service. In the third phase, when we determined firm capabilities, we considered the best department fit for a new service. Once the new service has been assigned to a department, responsibility can then be delegated to an individual within that group. This service coordinator will work with the firm's partners to answer additional questions.

What policies must be modified or instituted to support the service?

What will be the fee for the service?

What will be the budget for marketing the new service?

Once these questions have been answered, a preliminary budget should be prepared. This budget will cover all costs of introducing the new service including: (1) cost of staff training; (2) cost of additional staff needed to support the service; (3) budget available for marketing tools, such as a brochure or a seminar; and (4) break-even cost of providing the service. This analysis will help determine whether the new service can contribute to your firm's growth.

One of the most important elements in the service definition phase is to identify the individuals responsible for the new service. Optimally, they would include an accounting professional and a marketing professional. Minimally, the service coordinator should be an accounting or consulting professional who is given the appropriate time to coordinate the new service. All too often a new service with great potential is not successful because the individual assigned to the project did not have adequate coordination time.

*Phase 5: Coordinate the New Service.* Once the service has been defined, the newly appointed service coordinator must answer additional questions.

What staff will provide the service, and do they need additional training?

What staff will assist in promoting the service?

How can the service be marketed?

In addition, the coordinator must establish a timetable, personnel and material requirements and a follow-up/evaluation process. Coordination and control are important to ensure the success of the service plan. These tasks involve the next three phases of the service plan: (1) the marketing plan; (2) internal communications; and (3) evaluation and control.

*Phase 6: Develop the Marketing Plan.* Once you have defined your new service, you must develop a continuing program to communicate that your firm can provide this service. You will need to define: (1) the message; (2) the communications tools; and (3) the internal marketing support systems.

The service coordinator, along with the firm's marketing director or an outside marketing consultant, needs to design a marketing program to communicate to the targeted market how your firm's new service can meet the market's identified needs. Using the formal and informal research surveys, the service coordinator can identify the appropriate service message and the best way to communicate this message to your targeted market. In our personal financial planning example, current clients undoubtedly form part of this targeted market. Thus, in client service planning sessions, your professionals should develop action plans to let the firm's clients know about the availability of this service and its benefits.

Part of the service plan is to evaluate the marketing communications alternatives available to your firm, the most common of which are the following.

Public relations
    Seminars
    News releases
    Speeches
    Articles
    Publications
    Civic, social, community

Advertising
    Yellow pages
    Print
    Radio
    Television

Direct mail
    Newsletters
    Literature/Brochures
    Educational materials

Joint meetings
  Clients
  Prospects
  Referral sources
  Trade associations
  Sponsorships

Examine all the means available for communicating to your targeted market. Combine several of these alternative marketing methods, giving preference to the most efficient, cost-effective, and timely methods.

The service coordinator also must define the internal systems needed to support the marketing efforts for the new service. For example, if an advertising campaign is used, what is needed internally to ensure that telephone or mail inquiries are handled properly? Who should be receiving questions? Many marketing programs have failed because the internal systems were not developed to support the marketing efforts. Defining and developing the internal support systems is another important responsibility of the service coordinator.

***Phase 7: Develop an Internal Communications Plan.*** One of the most easily overlooked elements of the service plan is informing the staff of the new service. It is important to communicate to your staff what you are doing because they should understand the firm's services and because they can help sell the service. The following questions need to be addressed.

How do we communicate new services to our staff?
How do we enhance our staff's understanding of the new service?
How do we update our staff on new service developments?
How do we help our staff sell the new service?

To keep staff informed, an internal communication system needs to be developed. This can be a weekly newsletter that provides not only technical updates, but also notices about new services available, recent sales, and sales tips. It is essential that all staff, to varying degrees, be informed so that they are knowledgeable about the service when asked, or can identify a client in need of the new service.

*Phase 8: Evaluate Results.* The final phase of your service plan is to build in objectives that can be measured for both evaluation and control. Simply ask: How do we track the results of this new service? If the answer cannot be determined, then this is another task for the service plan coordinator. Who will track the results, and how?

In designing the tracking plan, it would be wise to set a timetable. Your first one may be a "guesstimate," but your ability to estimate will improve each time you develop or revise a plan. When can you expect results? Although marketing cannot create results overnight, if a concentrated marketing effort is taking place in June, July, and August, preliminary results may be observable in the fall. In addition to tracking results for the firm, the service coordinator should conduct follow-up surveys with clients to ascertain their satisfaction with the service, as well as ways to improve the firm's delivery systems. Table 2-1 illustrates related questions that need not only answers, but also an action plan.

*A Service Plan Focuses Your Efforts.* Each of the eight phases requires partner commitment, as well as a resource commitment to properly manage the service offering. The complete plan represents a management tool to use during the ongoing service delivery process. Table 2-2 presents a sample service plan for personal financial planning. In reviewing this sample, you will note that:

1. Concrete goals are presented so that progress can be evaluated.
2. Efforts are directed to a set number of activities.
3. Action steps follow clearly from the plan.
4. Research guides the planners in specific directions.

You will also see that a service plan need not be lengthy.

## TABLE 2–2. SAMPLE PLAN: PERSONAL FINANCIAL PLANNING SERVICE

### Service Plan
### Personal Financial Planning (PFP)
### Service Coordinator: KS

*Market Situation*

Based on information gathered through both a formal and an informal survey, three markets have been identified for personal financial planning services; they are:

1. Clients and potential clients whose gross income exceeds $50,000 and net worth exceeds $250,000. The estimated number of clients fitting into this category is between 150 and 175.
2. Business clients with 50 or more employees to whom the firm's financial planning services can be offered as an employee benefit. We have 40 clients in this category.
3. Referral sources with customers that fit into categories 1 and 2 above where the firm's financial planning services can be offered as a customer service. The firm currently serves 35 community banks that are targets for this service.

*Competitive Situation*

Many of our direct CPA competitors have not aggressively entered the personal financial planning services area. However, the major competitors are certified financial planners located in brokerage houses and insurance companies. We can take a position of promoting the independence of our PFP services because we sell no products directly as a result of the service.

*Firm Capability*

Our tax department currently provides comprehensive financial planning to key clients. In addition, we offer separate areas of personal financial planning, such as estate, education, and retirement planning. However, we have not organized these efforts into a packaged service. Also, KS has completed four parts of the six-part exam necessary to qualify as a Certified Financial Planner.

*Define the Service*

The personal financial planning service line will consist of two services: a comprehensive package and a component service that eventually would evolve into a comprehensive plan. For the comprehensive plan, clients would pay $1,000 to $3,000, depending on the plan's complexity. The component approach would be on a project-fee basis. For example, tax planning would be in a range of $150 to $300, depending on the complexity.

## Coordinate the Service

KS will be responsible for organizing and coordinating the PFP service. A special half-day training course will be given to all staff assistants, junior and senior accountants, and tax managers on the special procedures in PFP. At the partner/manager meeting in January, attendees will receive a manual containing the basic data questionnaire and material describing services and procedures. Staff assignment will be identical to other tax projects and controlled accordingly. One week prior to formal introduction of the service, the internal newsletter will describe the new service, and all new supporting materials will be attached to the newsletter.

## Market Plan

The primary market for the PFP service will be individual clients. Business clients and referral sources will be the secondary market.

### Goals
The primary goal of the PFP group in our first year is to perform comprehensive PFP plans for 40 individuals. The secondary goal is to begin various component PFP services to an additional 35 clients or prospects.

### Strategy
The message to communicate PFP services will be based on the theme "independent financial planning counsel." Two brochures will be developed—one describing the PFP planning process and the second, a case study of a PFP client. Seminars will be given in the spring and fall to individual clients and business-related clients. A direct mail campaign, using our firm's client newsletters, will also be used to reinforce PFP efforts.

### Timetable

| Topic/Audience | Month |
| --- | --- |
| Internal Training | January |
| Announcements/News Releases | February |
| Seminars | |
|   Clients (Individual) | March |
|   Referral sources | March |
|   Business group | |
|     Small business | April |
|     Manufacturing | April |
|   Clients (Individual) | September |
| Direct Mailings | |
|   Clients | April |
|   Business groups | |
|     Small business | May |
|     Manufacturing | May |
|     Small business | August |

**TABLE 2–2.** (Continued)

---

*Budget*
The budget for developing and implementing PFP per the above activities is $9,500.

*Internal Communication*

In addition to the activities described in "Coordinate the Service" (above), we will hold a one-hour seminar for all our staff to give them an introduction to the process. We also will offer them the service at cost so that they can describe the benefits they received as they talk with clients and prospects.

*Evaluate and Control Plan*

Our sales reporting system already contains a PFP code, so we will be able to track our progress. After six months, we will evaluate our performance against plan (40 comprehensive and 35 component plans). If we are not on track, we will take remedial action by formally structuring client service planning sessions around PFP.

---

# ☐ WHY INTEGRATE SERVICE PLANS?

The key part of the strategic marketing process is the integration of service plans. One major purpose of integrating service plans is to consolidate firm resources, both monetary and staff. An integrated plan should serve as the foundation of your marketing and service efforts. As opportunities for expanded services develop, you will be in a better position to evaluate their relationships with the other service offerings of your firm. The risk of developing unrelated or incompatible services is, therefore, minimized.

Through an integration process, your firm's strategic marketing plan takes form. Instead of each group or department functioning independently, integration of the various service plans can:

1. Communicate a consistent message widely.
2. Identify cross-selling opportunities.
3. Reduce marketing costs.
4. Consolidate personnel time commitments.

These four benefits are important to understand.

## Communicate a Consistent Message Widely

Maintaining consistency in your firm's image can be difficult if each of your service or group coordinators operates independently. This is particularly important if the coordinators are responsible for developing their own marketing materials. Without an integrated plan to coordinate the independent efforts, the firm's messages—and, therefore, its image—will be hard to control. Why is it important to have a consistent image? Like many of the services that your firm offers, there is an overlap in the business market that each service coordinator desires to reach. A consistent message will enhance the strength of the firm, while benefiting each service group.

## Identify Cross-Selling Opportunities

When integrating the service plans, you will identify a number of similar services and duplicative marketing efforts. You then can take steps to consolidate marketing efforts. In this manner, programs that are designed not only will meet the needs of clients, but also will benefit a number of service or group plans.

## Reduce Marketing Costs

The programs or materials developed in your firm should be designed so that they deliver a consistent message and benefit more than one client group or department. The result? Efficient use of your marketing dollars. For example, a personal financial planning seminar, developed in your new service plan, can be used for other target groups, such as health care or manufacturing clients. Start out with a standard seminar package, including invitations, checklists, and follow-up materials. Design supplemental materials tailored to suit each group's individualized needs. Developing programs or materials that can be used by a number of client groups will maximize your marketing efforts while minimizing costs.

## Consolidate Personnel Time Commitments

One of the most important benefits of integrating service plans is consolidating personnel commitments by maximizing effec-

tive use of time. For example, a direct mail brochure on personal financial planning can be used by a number of your client
groups. You are saving a service coordinator's time by using
the same material across several service groups. Client-oriented service coordinators will want to personalize this brochure for their respective market. To individualize this mailing
piece, the respective service coordinators can write a cover letter to their clients or prospects personalizing the information
for the industry group. The service coordinators, thus, save
time by not having to develop their own mailing piece; yet,
they are sending a client-oriented communication.

## Integrate Plans for Success

Many firms lose marketing effectiveness by developing individual service plans and, then, ignoring the importance or benefits
of integrating the plans. Only through integration of the service plans can your firm make strategic marketing an effective
process. In this way, you project a consistent message across
markets, while using the discipline of marketing effectively
and making efficient use of your professionals' valuable time.
Through consolidation, your firm will profit. A strategic plan is
an essential resource for the firm's survival and growth.

## □ HOW TO INTEGRATE SERVICE PLANS

One of the easiest ways to integrate service plans is to catego-
rize the various services and industry groups into a simple matrix. Using the simple matrix form in Table 2-3, start by filling
in the proposed marketing activities for one service group, in
this case the tax department, or an industry group (e.g., small
business clients). Plot the activities proposed for an entire year.

In Table 2-4, the activities for a firm's service and industry
group plans for the entire year have been filled in. Can the activities be planned to take full advantage of each group's marketing activities? As shown in Table 2-4, through the integration of marketing activities on this matrix, the potential for
interaction between groups becomes self-evident. Your market-

**TABLE 2–3. MARKETING MATRIX**

| Month | Firm Marketing | Tax Service Group | Small Business Industry Group |
|---|---|---|---|
| January | | | |
| February | | | |
| March | | | |
| April | | | |
| May | | | |
| June | | | |
| July | | | |
| August | | | |
| September | | | |
| October | | | |
| November | | | |
| December | | | |

ing activities will gain focus through use of this matrix approach. Whether you have one or two plans to integrate or many, this matrix should be a working tool to see where marketing activities can best be scheduled and how groups can interact effectively.

In the matrix in Table 2-5, we have integrated the plans of three service areas (corporate tax, personal financial planning, and management consulting services) and three industry groups (small business, health care, and manufacturing). The matrix shows how marketing activities and materials developed to support those services are used by the different industry groups and are supported by the firm's image-building activities—in this example, advertising and public relations.

## TABLE 2–4. SAMPLE MARKETING MATRIX: ONE SERVICE/ONE INDUSTRY

| Group | Firm Marketing | Tax Service Group | Small Business Industry Group |
|---|---|---|---|
| January | | Direct Mailing: Auto log Forms filing | Direct Mailing: Special report Forms filing |
| February | Schedule appointments with key tax and business clients | Speak at small business forum | Small business forum |
| March | Schedule appointments with key tax and business clients | | Direct Mailing: Follow-up year-end management services |
| April | | Invitation to seminar | Invitation to seminar |
| May | Seminar for Small Business Owners | Speak at seminar on tax implication of small business | Seminar for small business owners |
| June | | Write article on new tax changes | Seminar follow-up |
| July | | | |
| August | | Review key clients' tax planning needs Invitation to seminar | Invitation to seminar |
| September | Seminar: Key clients' tax planning needs | Booklet: Tax Changes Tax Planning Guide | Seminar: Key clients' tax planning needs Seminar follow-up |
| October | | Direct Mailing: Tax guides Joint meeting Key clients | Invitation to seminar on computers |
| November | Seminar: Computers | Direct Mailing: Last-minute tax savings tips | Seminar on computers Seminar follow-up Direct Mailing: Last-minute tax savings tips |
| December | | Open House: Holiday theme | |

Note how the strategy for marketing personal financial planning services (PFP) is integrated into programs across the matrix. If, for example, a PFP seminar is developed by the PFP service coordinator, it is supported by the firm through advertising and public relations programs. Further, the seminar is used by the industry groups at different times to maximize the firm's support. You can use the matrix, therefore, to plot out the various services or industry-group plans for the upcoming year and to identify common marketing resources. In this way, you can have several separate but interrelated plans which are coordinated with common marketing strategies and professional resources. This integrated approach is the most efficient way to allocate marketing dollars and manpower.

If your firm is client-centered, this matrix approach is superior in structuring the marketing efforts around the firm's actual services or "products," (e.g., tax, management consulting, personal financial planning). The strategic marketing plan not only mirrors the internal organization, it also reinforces it. Your firm will be structured to provide a wide range of services through its service groups, with each service group responsible for managing its service plan and delivering the services needed.

It is critical to recognize the extent to which the integration of service plans can drive and expand the marketing activities of the firm—whether paid media, public relations opportunities, training seminars, or controlled and targeted mailing programs. Your firm's success hinges on the way you structure its activities to support programs as effectively as possible. This consistency, repetition, and reinforcement will make the whole far greater than the sum of the parts. A strategic marketing plan delivers results precisely because it is so multifaceted.

## ☐ STRATEGIC MARKETING BUILDS ON SERVICE EXCELLENCE

Strategic marketing helps you and your partners manage your practice and your client relationships. In the development of a

**TABLE 2–5. SERVICE PLAN INTEGRATION MATRIX**

| | Firm | Services | | | Industry Groups | | |
|---|---|---|---|---|---|---|---|
| | Advertising and PR Programs | Tax-Corporate Service Coordinator: WTY | Personal Financial Planning (PFP) Service Coordinator: KS | Management Consulting Service Coordinator: LC | Small Business Service Coordinator: VL | Health Care Service Coordinator: RAS | Manufacturing Service Coordinator: RUD |
| January | Personal financial planning theme Computer theme | Direct mailing: Auto logs Forms filing | Introduction/ Training | | Direct mailing: Special report Forms filing | Direct mailing: Special report | Direct mailing: Special report Forms filing |
| February | Personal financial planning theme Computer theme | Speak at small business forum | | Direct mailing: Record keeping Inventory Facilities management Computer studies | Bimonthly mailing: Emphasize PFP | Bimonthly mailing: Emphasize computer | Key client forum |
| March | Personal financial planning theme Computer theme | | Seminar: PFP Clients Referral sources | Exhibit at Computer Fair | Direct mailing: Follow-up Year-end Management Services | Direct mailing: Computer studies | |
| April | Personal financial planning theme Computer theme | | Direct Mailing: PFP info Case study Checklist | Seminar: Computers for better management | Seminar: Financial Planning Bimonthly mailing | Bimonthly mailing: Emphasize PFP | Direct mailing: Personal financial planning: Case study |
| May | Personal financial planning theme Computer theme | | | | Open House Direct Mail: Follow-up letter to seminar attendees and nonattendees | Seminar: Financial planning | Key client forum Topic: PFP |

| Month | | | | | | |
|---|---|---|---|---|---|---|
| June | | Write article on new tax changes | | Bimonthly mailing Miniseminar: PFP for client employees | Bimonthly mailing Open House Direct mailing: Financial planning case study | Direct mailing: Facilities management Miniseminar: PFP for client employees |
| July | | | | | | |
| August | Tax changes Computers and Business | Review: Key clients' tax planning needs | Seminar: Computers for: commercial health care | Direct mailing: Financial planning case study Bimonthly mailing | Bimonthly mailing Direct mailing: New tax changes article | Key client golf outing Direct mailing: New tax changes |
| September | Tax changes Computers and business | Booklet: Tax changes | Seminar: Tax and financial planning | Direct mailing: Nonprofits and automation | Direct Mailing: Facilities management | Direct mailing: New tax changes article |
| October | Tax changes Computers and business | Direct mailing: Tax guides Joint meetings with key clients | | Seminar: Computers for better management Bimonthly mailing | Bimonthly mailing | Seminar: Computers for better management |
| November | Tax changes Computers and business | Direct mailing: Last-minute changes for tax savings | Direct mailing: Last-minute changes for tax savings | Direct mailing: Last-minute changes for tax savings | Seminar: Computers for health care | Key client forum Direct Mail: Last-minute changes for tax savings |
| December | Direct mailing: Holiday card | Direct mailing: Holiday card | Direct mailing: Holiday card | Bimonthly mailing Direct mailing: Holiday Card | Direct mailing: Holiday card | Direct mailing: Holiday card |

service plan, as well as in the integration of service plans, marketing and client service are interrelated.

First, a service plan in based on an understanding of client needs and values—from the client's point of view. Many professionals approach client service asking, "What service would I want if I were in this situation?" This question is *not* client oriented. The client-oriented professional asks, "What service would I want if I were the client in this situation?" This professional tries to put himself into the client's situation or frame of reference as if he were the client. *As if* is the critical factor. Understanding of client needs correlates directly with success in selling additional services and inversely with many failures in new service development. Further, understanding of client satisfaction allows professionals to hone their service delivery systems to ensure that clients remain clients.

Second, strategic marketing forces you to use the discipline of marketing. Developing a service involves an orderly process in which each step is challenged. Planning and research are basic to service development. Every related area is considered, including training, communications, and client service planning. Service plan integration forces you to set direction and priorities. Programs which are consistent with and supportive of your firm's long-term goals dominate your matrix. Activities which do not support these goals are readily apparent and, thus, can be rejected without wasting resources on evaluation. You will have a sound basis to say, "No," to requests that are unrelated to your firm's goals.

Third, strategic marketing involves the firm's resources, its people, in an organized way so that they spend their marketing time effectively and efficiently. For example, if a number of service plans require staff training, they can be consolidated into one session, instead of time-consuming minisessions. Each service coordinator will know what responsibilities are assigned and who is available to assist in the implementation phases. Each person at every staff level will understand his/her responsibilities. In strategic marketing, everyone in the firm plays a role in marketing. Thus, as people progress in their careers, marketing is accepted, even embraced, as part of their job descriptions and of their professional commitment. The end result is effective use of a firm's most important asset—its staff.

Finally, strategic marketing can yield measurable results, whether an increase in revenues, professional commitment, client satisfaction, or general awareness of the firm. The process is there to be implemented and refined, and checkpoints can be built in to ensure that you stay on course.

Accountants who truly market understand that client-oriented service is the core of marketing in a professional service firm. They understand that being a client-centered professional is one of the most challenging, demanding, and creative positions in business today. They also know that the accounting profession must attract many more people who have the interpersonal, technical, and business skills and abilities required. Accountants who truly market create, among their clients, a predisposition to buy because these professionals have communicated their involvement and understanding and deliver the services clients need and value.

## ☐ NOTE

1. See Bishea, Meile & Associates, Inc., "Opinion Study for the Wisconsin Institute of Certified Public Accountants" (Milwaukee, Wisconsin: July 21, 1982).

# PART TWO

# HOW TO ADMINISTER FOR RESULTS

# 3

## HOW TO ORGANIZE YOUR MARKETING RESOURCES

The complement of strategic planning is implementation. Your plans may be well thought out, but making them work is what counts, what yields results. The people who drive the process of implementing marketing programs are key to their success. Thus, your firm must have top-notch people providing the leadership and support to help your partners and professionals be successful in their marketing activities.

Specifically, you must decide first who in the firm will be responsible for developing the marketing effort. Whether your practice is small or large, the responsibility for establishing its marketing policies must belong to a partner. Then you must decide who will be responsible for implementing the marketing plan. Depending on your firm's goals and needs, you may want to develop a marketing function within the firm. That development process is the focus of this chapter. The following chapters concern consulting resources which can assist you with program development and implementation.

### ☐ WHAT ARE YOUR ORGANIZATIONAL OPTIONS?

The development of the marketing function involves two major considerations. First are the marketing positions possible; second is the applicability of these positions to your firm's situation. Then, you must weigh the available options.

## The Marketing Positions

Many firms have assigned responsibility for the marketing program to a partner, sometimes referred to as the partner in charge of marketing. In smaller firms, the managing partner usually fulfills this role. This individual usually has little, if any, marketing education or experience. Therefore, he must depend upon outside marketing consultants for direction in developing true marketing plans for the firm. In some instances, this approach has been successful; in others, it has not. Success has come when the marketing partner is well respected by his peers for his client service strength and when he has been released from other responsibilities to spend 75 percent or more of his time in the role.

Many firms are unable to make this great a commitment of partner involvement. Realizing that marketing is a vital function, they have tried other alternatives, including hiring: (1) a marketing director; (2) a marketing coordinator; or (3) an administrative assistant. Table 3-1 summarizes the four positions in terms of education and experience requirements, as well as responsibilities. Let's examine the differences in these positions.

A marketing or communications director's major responsibilities would be to define the direction, strategies, and structure of the firm's marketing activities. This management-level person has five to eight years' experience in business marketing and has an advanced degree in marketing, communications, or a related field.

The marketing coordinator would operate as the quarterback of a firm's marketing activities. Once the direction has been defined, the coordinator would be responsible for implementing, controlling, and tracking marketing programs. The required educational background is a degree in business, marketing, or communications, and three to five years' experience in business or a service industry.

**TABLE 3–1. MARKETING POSITIONS WITHIN ACCOUNTING FIRMS**

| Marketing Position | Education | Experience | Responsibilities | Stand-Alone Position: Use of Outside Consultants (Advertising/PR) | Resource Combinations | | | |
|---|---|---|---|---|---|---|---|---|
| | | | | | Optimal | Workable | Minimal | Unworkable |
| Partner in charge—Marketing (PCM) | Degree in accounting | CPA; over 10 years in profession | Sets policy; informs marketing professionals of firm needs; supports marketing efforts | Generally no experience or training in marketing; must rely on consultants for direction to define marketing plans | MD+MC+MA (V) or MD+MA (IV) | MD (I) or MC+Outside Consultant (II) | Outside Consultant | MA (III) |
| Marketing/Communications director (MD) | Advanced degree in marketing (MBA, MS) | From 5 to 8 years with business or service organization(s) | Defines strategies, programs, internal support systems; gives direction to firm objectives | Collaborates with outside consultants as needed | PCM+MA (IV) or PCM+MC (IV) | PCM+Support Staff (I) | PCM (I) | Working alone |
| Marketing coordinator (MC) | Degree in business (BAA, (BS, BA) | From 3 to 5 years of business experience | Coordinates and monitors ongoing marketing program | Requires direction of outside consultants as resources | PCM+MD+MA (V) or PCM+MD (IV) | PCM+Outside Consultant (II) | Outside Consultant | Working alone |
| Marketing/Administrative assistant (MA) | No degree required | From 3 to 5 years in administrative position | Aids in the administration and details of marketing program | Can only administrate details of programs; interaction with consultants minimal | Must be guided by upper-level planning and strategy formation | | | |

The marketing or administrative assistant would not have a marketing-related degree, but may have business experience as an assistant or an executive secretary. Responsibilities include monitoring marketing programs, as well as handling the details and follow-up responsibilities of these activities. This individual may have been with the firm and understands its services and functions, and, thus, would require minimal supervision once the responsibilities have been defined.

Without any guidance, firms have tried to use one or more of these positions to meet their marketing needs. Creating any one position has its advantages and drawbacks, as discussed in the next section. As we shall see, different resource combinations yield quite different results.

## Identifying the Resource Options

If a firm decides that only one position is necessary, what are its options? Actually, the firm has only one: a partner must be in charge of marketing. In a partnership, few efforts succeed without the interest, guidance, and power of a partner. Further, a partner must be involved for policy and guidance if any one of the other three positions is created. Both large and small practices have found that the managing partner is an especially effective leader of the marketing effort, particularly in the early stages.

If the partner position is the only one created, outside marketing consultants would most likely be used to help define the appropriate marketing strategies. Firms taking this route have found the costs high, particularly if plans are not implemented. Failure to implement often results because the partner in charge of marketing has other professional and client obligations, and marketing is not his primary responsibility.

A firm does have other options—selecting combinations of individuals. What is the best alternative? Examining the possibilities, shown in Table 3-1, we find five seemingly workable resource combinations.

*Combination I: Partner in Charge of Marketing and Marketing/Communications Director.* If a firm selects this combination, the results will be a marketing management team combining the experience of the accounting profession with the expertise of marketing. To implement programs and projects, the marketing director would delegate responsibilities, including coordination, to accounting professionals and support staff.

*Combination II: Partner in Charge of Marketing and Marketing Coordinator.* This team combines knowledge of the accounting profession with implementation capability, and uses outside consultants, such as marketing consultants or public relations organizations, to provide the marketing expertise needed to define marketing programs. The marketing coordinator, with the support of the partner in charge of marketing, is responsible for implementing the plan. Once the planning process has been structured, the coordinator often can develop similar programs for the firm. Many firms have opted for this combination.

*Combination III: Partner in Charge of Marketing and Marketing Assistant.* This combination seems attractive because the assistant can be drawn from the firm's support staff. Thus, both team members know the firm's players and procedures. Also attractive is the low, if any, increase in overhead. However, selecting this combination could have a negative effect on marketing programs. Neither person has the necessary experience or training to define the marketing elements that create successful results for the firm. Thus, they operate by trial and error. Unless marketing consultants play an active role in the definition, implementation, and evaluation of marketing activities, this team will fail.

*Combination IV: Partner in Charge of Marketing, Marketing Director, and Marketing Coordinator;* or *Partner in Charge of Marketing, Marketing Director, and Marketing Assistant.* A firm that selects this combination is well on its way toward developing a marketing department. Working as a team, the partner in charge of marketing and the marketing director define objectives, strategies, and processes for achieving their firm's marketing goals. They are not dependent on outside resources. When outside resources are used, the marketing director manages the relationship. The marketing coordinator or assistant assists with the implementation process and details required for a successful program.

*Combination V: Partner in Charge of Marketing, Marketing Director, Marketing Coordinator, and Marketing Assistant.* The optimal combination would include the four marketing positions, functioning within a firm as a formal marketing department. This configuration represents the marketing organization of the future. It is not a reality today. The degree and level of marketing sophistication would equal that of corporate marketing organizations.

## Weighing the Options

Today, many accounting firms are considering which level of marketing experience best suits their needs. In both the short and long run, selecting marketing professionals may save the firm costly consulting fees, while making marketing work and achieving measurable results. The resources your firm invests in marketing should align with your firm's needs in both the management of the marketing effort and the implementation of specific programs.

## ☐ HOW TO MANAGE THE MARKETING FUNCTION

Establishing marketing policy is the responsibility of the partner in charge of marketing or the practice's managing partner, when there is no partner directing the function. Defining strategies, designing support systems, and other management responsibilities may be carried out by the partner in charge of marketing or the marketing director.

One of the roles played by marketing management is that of the facilitator who makes it easier for professionals to develop marketing programs and activities. The facilitating role is especially important in market planning, whether for a practice, an industry, or a new service. Peter Horowitz, the director of marketing with Coopers & Lybrand in Canada, describes his application of the facilitator role to a critical marketing activity, the office market planning process.

The next section focuses on another responsibility of marketing management: defining marketing programs and systems to support the marketing plan. The programs associated with internal marketing are particularly important because client consciousness is critical in a client-oriented service organization. Raising the consciousness of professionals and support staff is the focus of the subsequent section, "Managing Internal Marketing Programs," by Maureen Broderick, the marketing manager with Price Waterhouse in San Francisco, and John Schiffman, a partner with Smith, Batchelder & Rugg in Hanover, New Hampshire.

---

## FACILITATING THE MARKET PLANNING PROCESS
*Peter M. Horowitz*
*Coopers & Lybrand, Canada*

The market planning program developed at Coopers and Lybrand is a process that, in effect, has no magic to it and is not particularly unique. It is a process of self-discovery and sensitization, a process developed to introduce marketing planning to the smaller practice office. Such an office is one that has anywhere from six to fourteen partners, with a proportional number of professionals and administrative staff.

### Background

There has been a substantial growth in the market share of the major international firms, which now do the audits of 99 percent of the large corporations (publicly and privately held) in Canada. There has been much discussion over the kinds of restrictions that are imposed on the profession by the provincial institutes of chartered accountancy. The rules have eased for Canadian accountants in a *de facto* way; that is, as rules have been ignored, they have fallen away. And, as the environment in which accountants practice has become more competitive, provincial regulatory bodies have had to alter the rules of practice to reflect increasingly common marketing activities, such as advertising. There are still some restrictions that remain in effect. They are as follows.*

1. Accounting firms are not permitted to indulge in "self-laudatory" puffery in advertising.
2. Accounting firms cannot use the term "specialist" in any way. For example, a firm cannot refer to its professionals as specialists in taxation.
3. An accounting firm cannot endorse commercial products. For example, the managing partner could not appear in an advertisement for Apple computers.
4. An accounting firm cannot solicit directly or indirectly the clients of another firm. This rule is being violated every day. There is still some sensitivity to such a practice. It has not stopped anyone from having lunch with another firm's client. However, the amount of cold calling is limited. Canadian accounting firms are careful about overt solicitation practices.

In spite of these restrictions, the competitive environment is very hot in Canada. A tremendous amount of pressure is centered on the fee structure. Lowballing is increasingly common. For example, we submitted a proposal for a major public sector audit. We estimated the job at full fee rates to be $250,000; we submitted a bid for $175,000 which we saw as reasonable and competitive. Another firm won the bid with a $95,000 fee commitment. In 1981, Coopers & Lybrand produced 60 major proposals; this number grew to 175 in 1983 and to 300 in 1985.

There are 22 Coopers offices across the country and over 250 partners. Each office operates independently; there is no national pooling of revenues. For a number of years, every Coop-

*Editors' note. These restrictions apply in Canada. Check with local regulatory agencies to determine what restrictions apply to your firm.

ers office has been required to go through an annual planning cycle. A part of this cycle has been the development of an office action plan. Recently, this planning process revealed that in every office the partners were aware of the need to react to an increasingly competitive environment. However, there was little sense of how they might proceed with the development of a coordinated, more aggressive plan.

At that time, I was asked by the Ontario region of the firm to develop a program that would help the Ontario offices galvanize themselves to solve this problem. The regional partner was contemplating a written document—a guidebook. My view was that practice offices did not need another sheaf of papers; instead, they needed a process that would be both a learning process in itself and a self-sustainable marketing planning tool.

## Problem

The main issue was to convert an awareness of increased competition into planned and effective marketing activity without creating undue discomfort. Such discomfort derives from a view of sales as unprofessional and a notion that aggressive marketing is inconsistent with the accountant's professional self-image.

## Assumptions

Three key assumptions were made in developing the program.

1. Market intelligence is resident in each practice office but is neither organized nor shared.
2. The process of developing a marketing orientation is perhaps more important than the plan itself.
3. Marketing is most effective at the operational level.

The first assumption was that partners in any given office know a lot more about their market and marketing than they believe they do. Market information in the practice office tends to be disorganized and not shared in any coherent way. Secondly, the process is more important than the final product itself, although it should produce a tangible result. People expect that when they put time into a project they will have something to show for it. Finally, marketing awareness and marketing skills must be developed and implemented at the operational level.

To summarize these assumptions, marketing must be inner-directed. It must be consistent with the self-image of the practice and must function on an operational level. A process for a group of partners and managers to improve self-awareness and formulate strategies can result in a concrete and modest plan of attack to cover a 12-month period.

## Marketing Action Planning Process

The purpose of the marketing action planning process is for participants to learn about their market and themselves in a coordinated and organized way, to learn about their environment, to share information about competitors, and then to move into a process of formulating marketing strategy and structured marketing activities.

*Ground Rules.* First, there were rules relating to: (1) partner commitment; (2) practice-office commitment; (3) informal seminar style; and (4) role of the facilitator.

The first rule concerned the requirement of partner commitment. Partners could not delegate responsibility (i.e., no skipping of meetings). This commitment is essential to any kind of learning process. If you do not have it, you will not progress.

The second rule was that the practice office had to make a commitment to conduct marketing research. The national office would not perform the work for them. It was something that could not be undertaken by anyone outside the office.

The third rule was that the program would be informal and that discussion would be frank and open. The program would not succeed with hype.

Finally, I would serve as the facilitator of this process, not its director. I did not chair the sessions; I simply helped chart their direction.

The program consisted of an introductory meeting of two hours in which we talked about what we were going to do. Then there were three seminars, of five to six hours each, at about two-week intervals. In between the seminars the office conducted its research, which formed the basis for discussion at the subsequent session.

The production of the marketing action plan was the culmination of this process, the tangible symbol of the learning, information-gathering, and assessment process.

A key point to bear in mind is that, from start to finish, the practice office "owns" the marketing action program. It is not viewed as a "national" activity superimposed on the local partners. No report to senior management is required; accountability remains within the practice office.

***Role of the Facilitator.*** My role as a facilitator was (1) to function as an interested but disinterested insider-outsider in order to keep sessions on track; (2) to offer alternatives, options, choices; (3) to ask hard questions occasionally; and (4) to provide an overview of what was being accomplished and reminders of what needed to be done. At times, it was necessary to restrain enthusiasm in order to maintain a focus on activities that were well-defined and achievable. Additionally, it was my responsibility to ensure that the process moved toward the goal of analysis and strategy development while keeping practicality and achievability always in full view.

## The Marketing Action Program

### Phase I: Market/Environment Assessment

Territory
Market profile

Influences—economic, social, political, technical

Changing client attitudes and requirements

The first phase of the marketing action program consists of a fairly detailed market assessment conducted entirely by the practice office. This assessment includes a precise definition of the geographical mandate of the practice and the gathering and analysis of market data drawn from local sources. The assessment is expected to include a community economic profile with a careful look at future economic prospects, demographic trends, and projected changes in the composition of the economic base. One such analysis revealed that, although an office was centered in an economically depressed area with little economic growth predicted, its geographical mandate included an adjacent region marked by rapid industrial development. This region had been virtually ignored by the practice in the past. Another practice office discovered that manufacturing activity outside the major population center of its territory was far higher than expected. In both cases, this new information resulted in significant changes in outlook and had a fairly dramatic impact on short- and long-term marketing strategies.

In addition to examining the market and critical influences that are exerted on it (e.g., plant closings, union activity, political change, and concurrent growth or reduction in government services), the environment analysis phase requires the practice to assess client attitudes and demands for services. Some practice offices noted a high degree of loyalty on the part of audit clients; other markets were characterized by frequent auditor change as a fee reduction strategy.

The positive result of the first phase of the marketing action program is the security and confidence that knowledge, gathered and shared, produces. Each practice office seemed more confident of its future having fully defined the economic characteristics, patterns, and projections for its territory. The market/environmental analysis phase provides an effective backdrop for further analysis and strategy development, as it ensures that all participants are operating within a common information context.

## Phase II: Office Profile

Current client base

Current resources/expertise/marketing activities

Aspirations and objectives

Phase II requires the practice office to engage in some organized and constructive navel-gazing, to take the time to be constructively introspective. In this phase, the analysis of the current client base is critical. Patterns emerge from such an analysis which not only affect how a practice views itself, but also lay the experiential foundation for future marketing strategies. One practice discovered that, although it tended to view itself in the context of its four major clients, nearly 70 percent of the client base consisted of smaller, owner-managed, entrepreneurial entities. Another discovered that 30 percent of its annual billings derived from the construction industry. A third realized that its client base gave it a valid claim to expertise in the transportation and communications industries.

This client-base analysis is accompanied by a hard and critical look at the resources and expertise resident in the practice. In some cases, expertise is identified as being available but underutilized; in others, certain expertise is desirable but absent. In most cases, a review of current marketing activities reveals an understandable emphasis on personal, nondirected contact-building, on advertising that has developed sporadically without an overall objective, and more often than not, on *ad hoc* attempts to raise the profile of the practice with little follow-through.

## Phase III: Competitor Analysis

Who they are

Their strengths and weaknesses

Their apparent marketing strategies

Each practice is asked to identify and analyze its key competitors. Information concerning competitors, although usually accurate, is most often conveyed anecdotally. Competitor analysis should structure this informal information in a way that brings it into clear focus. The competitor analysis phase tends to identify, by comparison, the weaknesses of the practice itself, particularly with respect to marketing activities, industry expertise and the community profiles of key partners. Equally important, it frequently reveals that other firms are often no better situated strategically to capitalize on growth opportunities.

The completion of the first three phases—market, office profile, and competition—prepares the practice for the next, and perhaps most critical, phase: the strategy formulation stage. Here, the characteristics of the market, the resources of the practice, and the strengths and weaknesses of the competition must be sifted to reveal growth opportunities. From the point of view of process, what has been achieved thus far is the creation of a common body of knowledge and a shared vocabulary, which is, perhaps, atypical of the professional practice.

### Phase IV: Strategy Formulation

Opportunities and threats

Strategy options

Drawing tentative conclusions

It is only possible to develop an effective marketing strategy against a backdrop of coherent market information. Thus, the first three phases of the marketing action program are really preparation for the identification of growth opportunities. Phase IV, which is less structured and less research-oriented than the earlier phases, asks the practice office to assess the information previously gathered, and to highlight gaps in the market, geographical areas with significant growth potential, target clients, current clients who might be at risk. This part of the process leads the practice through an examination of how it can capitalize on its strengths, take into account its weaknesses, and operate productively within a competitive context.

The matrix in Table 3-2 describes the four major strategy op-

**TABLE 3–2. STRATEGY OPTIONS**

|                 | Current Services                          | New Services                          |
| --------------- | ----------------------------------------- | ------------------------------------- |
| Current Clients | Selling current services to current clients | Selling new services to current clients |
| New Clients     | Selling current services to new clients    | Selling new services to new clients    |

tions available to a practice. The least expensive, and thus potentially most profitable, strategy involves selling additional current services to existing clients. The most expensive option is the development of new services of interest principally to new clients. The matrix was used to highlight the appropriateness and desirability of particular opportunities as they were identified and described.

The discussion in Phase IV leads to a list of strategic growth opportunities, which is then narrowed down to a group of achievable marketing objectives. In one instance, a practice office identified 16 such growth opportunities. Recognizing that not all could be achieved over the 12-month life of the marketing action program, the group, through discussion and evaluation, selected eight high-priority objectives and built the marketing plan around those. In another case, a practice office agreed to attack five objectives over a nine-month period and, then, to reassess its marketing situation to determine whether additional marketing objectives should be set.

### Phase V: Operational Planning

Objectives

Specifics, specifics, specifics

The final phase of the marketing action program takes the growth opportunities selected for implementation, frames them as concrete objectives, and then defines the specific actions that the office will undertake to achieve those objectives. It is in this phase that the facilitator takes the most active role, by suggesting those marketing tools which might be most effective in particular circumstances, by relating the local office's objectives to national strategies and by indicating where national marketing support can be provided. To be successful, the end result, the marketing action plan, must be concrete and highly specific. In addition, responsibility for each marketing activity must be assigned, with a deadline, to a specific individual. Each item in the plan must be defined in terms of:

1. What it will achieve
2. How it will be done
3. Who will do it
4. When it will be completed

The higher the degree of specificity, the greater the chances of success.

## Results

Once the marketing plan is constructed, the program is complete. It is then the responsibility of the practice office to implement the plan, and the facilitator becomes an ongoing advisor and provider of support. Success of the program is measured in two ways. One, obviously, is the practice office's ability to carry forward the implementation in achieving the objectives the plan contains. The second is the extent to which the practice adopts and sustains a marketing orientation, which is essential in a competitive environment. By both measures, the Coopers & Lybrand Marketing Action Program may be judged a success.

## MANAGING INTERNAL MARKETING PROGRAMS

*Maureen Broderick*
*Price Waterhouse, San Francisco*
*and*
*John T. Schiffman*
*Smith, Batchelder & Rugg, Hanover, NH*

An internal marketing program is designed to enhance the marketing abilities and activities of a firm's professionals and to motivate them to participate in the marketing efforts of the firm. Without an effective internal marketing program, your external marketing efforts will not be successful. The key to an effective internal marketing program is communication, which is the subject of the first section. The next two sections concern those aspects of internal marketing which focus on the firm's professionals: recruiting and motivation to market the firm's services. The emphasis on the firm's professionals is deliberate: People drive the firm's marketing programs.

## Building Communication Networks

The most important component of a successful internal marketing program is communication. All of your firm's professionals must understand the firm's objectives, marketing strategies, and plans. If they do not have this information, they cannot be expected to participate fully. This seems like a simple matter, but, in fact, communication is one of the weakest links in many firms. In part, this problem is caused by the dynamic nature of marketing and the continuous demand for information exchange. Identifying information needs and meeting these needs are two primary responsibilities of a firm's marketing management.

One of the tools many firms use successfully is the internal marketing newsletter, which serves as an ongoing communication vehicle. An internal newsletter can keep people abreast of new developments and areas of service on which the firm is focusing. More importantly, it gives recognition to people who are participating in the marketing effort.

Another approach is to use the firm's normal meeting structure as a communication springboard. For example, when departments or other groups have meetings, review the agenda to be sure that marketing topics are discussed. These may include new services, services provided by other departments or groups, new marketing tools, and sales ideas. Keeping everyone abreast of developments across the firm helps professionals be better marketers.

Client service planning meetings offer another means of communicating important information. In addition to the marketing director, all audit, tax and consulting staff who are involved with the client should attend. The purpose of the meetings is to discuss services currently being performed for clients in order to identify problem areas which need attention or any opportunities for additional services. These meetings should be held quarterly.

Staff orientation meetings and manuals can be used to introduce new personnel to marketing. These vehicles provide an overview of the firm's marketing program and the resources available.

Staff training in marketing is also an important element of communication. Many firms have not yet invested in marketing skills training. Learning marketing and sales skills in an organized, disciplined way, rather than a hit-or-miss way, produces increased growth and profits in the long run. Selling skills and oral presentation skills classes can be brought in-house and tailored to the specific needs of your staff. It is important to reinforce these training sessions with success stories in your office newsletter, as well as with occasional reminder memos on the importance of using the skills learned in the classes.

Staff evaluations also serve as a communication tool. It is not only important for the professional to discuss client experiences, but also to learn how to participate in the firm's marketing program. This critical area is discussed more fully in the section: "Motivating Professionals to Market."

For any given firm, the structure of the internal communication program relates to the firm's size. The smaller your firm, the more easily people communicate, thus increasing the likelihood of marketing success. If your firm is larger or has several locations, its communication needs and potential problems escalate. However, efforts to meet these needs and to promote more interaction pay off, and the major thrust of your firm's internal marketing program should focus on communication.

## Recruiting for Marketing

The marketing of accounting services has evolved dramatically in recent years in many areas. This increased emphasis has ramifications for an accounting firm's recruiting program. Where once a firm sought the technically proficient graduate, now the recruiting effort is directed at aggressive, growth-oriented individuals.

Today accounting firms find that the professionals who are comfortable with marketing are in short supply. We find that many people leave public accounting after the second year. This suggests that the criteria we are using in the recruiting process are not defined correctly and that we in accounting firms have not communicated our expectations regarding marketing participation to candidates, college and university professors, and, possibly, recruiters. A firm's recruiting and marketing directors must agree on the selection criteria for new professionals. Marketing professionals should become involved in the recruiting process, perhaps by interviewing candidates. This would communicate to candidates that marketing is important to the practice.

Today's recruits not only must be technically qualified, but also must have strong communication and interpersonal skills. If individuals want to get ahead in the firm, they must understand early the importance marketing will play in their advancement.

## Motivating Professionals to Market

If a firm's professionals accept the premise that marketing pervades the practice, we should be able to retain marketing-oriented professionals who satisfy clients and expand services. In this section, we address three topics. The first concerns ways to motivate partners, many of whom have long considered technical prowess to be the only indicator of service and are reluctant to participate in marketing activities. The second section focuses on motivating the professional staff to market. Generally younger staff are interested in broadening their experience, and our work with them should center on developing a structure in which they succeed. The third section concerns incentive systems.

*Motivating Partners.* Partners seem to fall into two groups. One is the "I have arrived" type; the other, the "I am arriving" type.

In marketing, the better type to deal with is the latter, because these partners understand the extremely competitive environment and the importance of working hard to keep the client. The "I am arriving" type gets involved, and partners in this category contribute to the marketing effort.

All partners should evaluate themselves and be evaluated by their fellow partners or by a partner in charge. This evaluation process can be used to determine the annual distribution of profits. Contribution to the marketing effort should be included in the evaluation system so that partners see a relationship between their individual marketing efforts and the firm's results.

***Motivating the Professional Staff.*** The evaluation of a professional's contribution to the firm must include marketing. Everyone should realize that your practice's system is designed to reward the individual who not only is a competent technician, but also excels at client service or at new business development. The reward must be one that not only yields a personal benefit, but also reinforces the activity so that the professional continues to contribute.

All staff should be evaluated on their marketing activities every six months. Each person should set a personal practice development plan of activities to be accomplished during the next six months. After six months, each person is evaluated on his accomplishments, and a new plan is developed. This process can often be difficult for newer staff who are unsure of their role in the marketing effort. The marketing professional can help by developing a list of marketing activities expected from each level of staff. New staff activities might simply be to stay involved with their alumni group, while a seasoned manager may be expected to speak at business functions, write articles, join clubs, and actively sell the firm's services.

The evaluator is an important person in the process, and it is critical to have evaluators who understand marketing. If your evaluation system has integrity, you must insist that evaluators, usually managers, have marketing skills and experience. Minimally, they should attend some type of marketing course before assuming evaluation responsibility.

Promotion is another strong motivator in a professional service firm. Advancement in your firm must depend on success in marketing. Define success at two levels: new client acquisition and expansion of services, and service to existing clients. It is commonly accepted now that professionals who are promoted to partner have demonstrated success in marketing.

Recognition is another strong motivator. Your firm's newsletters can be used to disseminate information about new clients and the people who participated in obtaining these clients. First, an article relates examples on how to sell work. Second, everyone learns who the successful marketers are. Professionals, particularly a senior or a staff associate, like to be recognized as a key member of the team that obtained a new client. Peer pressure plays an important part in increasing involvement.

Periodic sales meetings keep everyone informed about what is happening in marketing. Also, they provide an opportunity to recognize marketing leaders. At the meeting, people describe their activities—both achievements and plans, with the understanding that they are accountable for these plans at the next meeting.

*Using Incentive Programs.* Some firms are using cash or merchandise bonuses to motivate staff members to obtain new business. This approach is somewhat controversial. First, there is the argument that selling is part of every professional's responsibility, not an extra. Thus, there is no need for a special incentive. However, in practices where marketing responsibility is not ingrained, the sales bonus can be used effectively. The problem arises when a team effort results in a client gain and responsibility cannot be apportioned. The best approach is to design a system in which every contributor is rewarded.

An intraoffice contest for rewarding individuals can be a positive motivational tool. In Price Waterhouse, the San Francisco office's tax department needed a little motivational booster. We formed teams of approximately five or six people per team. The team that brought in the most new clients at the end of a six-month period won a prize—dinner, on the firm, at the restaurant of its choice. The teams worked very hard and brought in many more clients than they would have under normal conditions. Department morale was also boosted in this effort.

## Internal Marketing Makes a Difference

It is critical that partners recognize the importance of internal marketing programs in the firm's overall marketing effort. Only when all professionals understand the firm's objectives and plans can there be a concerted firmwide effort. Communication, then, is the most important factor in attaining this level of understanding. The role of the marketing professional is to define the communication needs and supporting systems.

Further, a firm's marketing and human resource functions are interdependent because the quality of a firm's professionals is directly related to the success of the firm's marketing effort. Thus, the marketing professional should play an active role in the recruiting process by defining appropriate selection criteria and by interviewing candidates. Marketing also is a key factor in the development of a firm's professionals. Thus, the marketing professional must devise programs that motivate professionals with rewards and reinforcements.

The overall result is that marketing can influence the culture of an accounting firm. Proper marketing efforts can focus a firm's attention on its publics and can also provide a degree of consistency and coherence to a firm's internal structure.

## ☐ HOW TO IMPLEMENT MARKETING PROGRAMS

To be successful, marketing programs must be coordinated and monitored continually. The administration of any marketing activity is a case study in detail. In fact, a total programmatic effort involves millions of details. It may be tempting to believe that your firm's marketing management—the partner in charge of marketing or the marketing director—can administer your firm's programs on a day-to-day basis. However, to assign implementation to management effectively diverts a lot of the manager's time from planning, strategy definition, and other critical areas. It is naive to conclude that a manager could devote only 10 percent or 20 percent of his time to implementation.

Implementation takes time—and special strengths, including coordination, follow-up, and systems building. In any given firm, the number of marketing-related administrative responsibilities is enormous. We believe these responsibilities are handled best by a marketing coordinator, a person who has three to five years of business experience in conjunction with a business degree.

Not only is the number of responsibilities large, but the responsibilities vary widely. The range and types of responsibility are described by Mary Hinkel in the following section, "Marketing Coordinator Responsibilities: A Cross Section." The director of marketing in the Atlanta office of Touche Ross, Hinkel analyzed the job descriptions of several marketing coordinators to develop this composite. You will find Hinkel's comments useful in identifying the specific responsibilities your firm needs to have covered so that your job description meets those needs. A word of caution: No single person can assume all the responsibilities Hinkel describes.

Who will succeed as a marketing professional? Our first response comes from Pamela Terry, who looked at her experience as the marketing coordinator in the Houston office of Touche Ross and identified four interpersonal skills areas as critical for success. Maureen Broderick, Price Waterhouse's marketing director in San Francisco, looked at success from a different perspective. She posed this question to a group of accounting and marketing professionals and summarized their responses in "Marketing Professionals Don't Fit a Mold."

Together, Hinkel, Terry, and Broderick provide a framework for understanding the demands associated with implementing marketing programs. This understanding is critical for firms which are introducing a marketing professional. If your firm has a marketing coordinator, their thoughts may give you some insights into restructuring or expanding that individual's responsibilities.

## MARKETING COORDINATOR RESPONSIBILITIES: A CROSS SECTION

*Mary S. Hinkel*
*Touche Ross, Atlanta*

The responsibilities of marketing coordinators are as diverse as the number of accounting firms across the country. However, these responsibilities seem to be concentrated in four basic marketing activities: (1) officewide; (2) individual staff members' needs; (3) marketing support systems; and (4) firm image, both external and internal. Each of these represents an area where marketing coordinators can play an important role in making your firm's marketing efforts successful.

### Officewide Marketing Activities

A marketing coordinator can develop, coordinate, and monitor marketing activities affecting major firm projects. Such projects include, but are not limited to: (1) client service programs; (2) industry programs; (3) targeted business programs; and (4) proposals and related presentations. Each of these activities represents a major firm marketing activity to be supported in both time and dollar commitments.

*Client Service Programs.* Client service programs generally center on those 20 percent of a firm's clients that represent 80 percent of its billings. Losing such clients would jeopardize the firm's bottom line. Activities, therefore, are directed toward these clients to maintain their loyalty to and dependence on your firm's services. The marketing coordinator ensures that the firm identifies the clients representing the top 20 percent. Once these clients have been identified, the marketing coordinator can determine whether the clients are receiving excellent service (e.g., if services are delivered promptly, if reports are being delivered on time, if additional services are needed). Recording information about the client and seeing that follow-up is defined and acted upon are other elements that a marketing coordinator can be responsible for in a client service program. Through coordination of these activities, the firm demonstrates that its services are client-oriented.

*Industry Programs.* As more accounting firms segment their services into industry groups, the marketing coordinator can play an important role coordinating industry-related events, such as developing industry mailing lists and routing important industry information to appropriate personnel. Through an effort to coordinate both materials and activities, a firm can avoid duplication within and among industry groups. Because the marketing coordinator is involved in each group, he can determine what the groups' common needs are and how they can be met. In this way, the groups will operate independently, but will be striving jointly toward the firm's business goals.

*Targeted Business Programs.* Another strategy many accounting firms are employing is the targeting of potential clients that either represent a new industry group or a specific, influential business. The marketing coordinator can assist with research, including key personnel, current attorney and banker, and size of business. This information is important not only in determining whether the business should be targeted, but also in formulating the strategy for meeting the target's decision makers. The marketing coordinator can also administer targeted business programs, making sure that the firm is visible and that contacts are frequent and pertinent.

*Proposals and Related Presentations.* Requests for proposals are more frequent today than ever before. As their frequency increases, so does the number of bidders. Therefore, the marketing coordinator's responsibility can include researching the appropriate industry, as well as evaluating the relevance of previous proposals. Once this information has been gathered, the marketing coordinator can also coordinate and monitor proposal preparation and production, including writing and editing where appropriate. The marketing coordinator also serves in the key role of "interpreter" of the technical information. Here the marketing coordinator assures that the message is client-oriented, not technically focused.

The marketing coordinator can be responsible for facilitating the various marketing activities of the firm to assure that they are client-oriented, that duplication of efforts is kept to a minimum, and that staff have the right information regarding these projects to assure these activities are successful.

## Individual Marketing Activities

Assisting the individual accounting professional, whether partner or staff, with marketing can be another responsibility for your marketing professional. A coordinator can support, monitor, coach, and coordinate all individual efforts so that everyone is contributing to the goals of the firm. Two areas in which the marketing coordinator can be particularly helpful are community involvement and contact programs.

*Community Involvement.* Accounting firms have always known the importance of community involvement. However, now that support of community activities has become commonplace, it is more important to maximize your firm's community exposure. The marketing coordinator can maintain information on community organizations within your market and advise which organizations are more influential than others. As a firm grows, it is also important to expand its visibility within the community by penetrating various influential organizations. The marketing coordinator can play an important role by tracking organizational involvement, matching staff to community organizations, and coordinating involvement within the community.

*Contact Programs.* To obtain maximum reach within the business community for your firm, the marketing coordinator can develop and maintain contact files for each professional. As the "quarterback," the marketing coordinator can make sure that the entire team is heading toward the goal—not all participating in a disorganized manner. How many times has a firm been embarrassed when two professionals contacted the same referral source with the identical letter? A marketing coordinator can oversee all activities and coordinate team efforts to avoid duplication.

Many marketing coordinators can work with individuals to increase their, and the firm's, visibility in the community. As such, the coordinator not only matches individuals with organizations, but also coordinates contacts within these groups to help solidify business relationships.

## Marketing Support Systems

The development of marketing support systems involves: (1) networking; (2) collateral coordination; (3) seminars; (4) alumni relations; and (5) marketing administration.

*Networking.* For firms with more than one office, a marketing coordinator can provide valuable network communication among offices and industry experts. In this way, the firm will have more technical resources than if each office worked independently. Shared expertise in industry groups can be very beneficial in expanding your client base.

*Firm Literature.* One of the most important elements of a firm's literature is consistency of image and theme. The marketing coordinator can look at the needs of each piece and help bring that consistency to printed materials, including stationery and newsletters. Another key factor in making your literature successful is an awareness of competitive materials. The marketing coordinator can obtain and evaluate these materials as they are developed.

One important element that is often overlooked is to use the literature developed in a coordinated and meaningful distribution program. Too often, firms spend a lot of money in the development stage and forget about distribution. How can a firm expect to receive a payback from the development of a brochure if it merely sits on the shelf or in a briefcase? One of the major roles of a marketing coordinator is to see that all materials developed by the firm are properly used.

**Seminars and Other Events.** Although many firms hold seminars (e.g., an annual tax seminar), there are sundry other topics that accountants are qualified to address. A marketing coordinator can identify topics not previously presented. Further, the marketing professional can coordinate the logistics and follow up for all firm presentations, whether firm sponsored or not. Setting up and publicizing a speaker's bureau is one way your firm's professionals can gain exposure in community and trade organizations, and this service could be organized by the marketing coordinator.

**Alumni Relations.** Many firms complain about the high turnover in staff; very few ever turn this somewhat negative reality into an opportunity. Alumni can be a source of new business because most alumni leave a CPA firm to go into a company in private industry. Here is an opportunity to get your foot in the door of that company. A marketing coordinator can develop an alumni program that reinforces a "positive" relationship between the alumni and your firm. Marketing coordinators can update and maintain directories of alumni, and plan and implement programs to build on a positive relationship, which may turn into client services.

**Marketing Administration.** There is an enormous number of systems that need to be developed within a firm so that marketing activities can be successful. For example, systems must be developed to establish and maintain mailing lists, and to track new and lost clients.

Coordinators can also assist departments in formulating marketing programs and plans. A library of marketing information on local businesses and markets should be maintained by the coordinator so that information is available to evaluate and pursue opportunities.

Marketing coordinators can be responsible for supporting all the marketing activities throughout the office. This would involve establishing a network or communication system between offices or departments, coordinating consistency in firm literature and other communication vehicles, and coordinating, monitoring and evaluating various seminar and alumni activities. To make a firm's marketing efforts successful, the marketing coordinator must be able to build the support systems needed.

## Enhance the Firm's Image

The marketing coordinator can have a positive effect on morale within a firm by (1) improving and maintaining internal and external communications, (2) expanding community exposure, and (3) training staff in marketing.

*Internal/External Communication.* Whether the marketing coordinator contributes to or edits firm publications, the image of the firm both externally and internally can be improved with positive and timely communication. Educating both clients and staff to the types and value of your firm's services can help attract new business. Marketing coordinators can create a positive image in the firm's communications by making sure all appropriate articles are client oriented.

*Community Exposure.* Public relations is one of the most important tools that a marketing coordinator has at his/her disposal. To gain access to the local press for the firm's professionals, the marketing coordinator should work with a local public relations firm, if applicable, or personally develop local media contacts. The marketing coordinator also can place promotional pieces, such as articles or news releases, in local newspapers and business journals for additional firm recognition.

*Staff Training.* Firms often use marketing coordinators for training professionals to be more market-oriented. Frequently we forget that all staff can contribute to the marketing efforts of the firm by participating in meetings, understanding firm services, and communicating this knowledge to clients, friends, peers, and acquaintances. With guidance from the marketing coordinator, professionals can assist the firm in increasing its visibility within the business community.

A marketing coordinator can help enhance your firm's image among your staff by increasing their knowledge of marketing and the firm. The coordinator can also obtain additional community exposure for the firm through public relations efforts and quality publications.

## Focus Activities for Success

The number of marketing professionals who have joined accounting firms throughout the country is increasing rapidly. Marketing coordinators can add to the marketing efforts of your accounting firm on a variety of levels, from officewide programs to individual staff training. These coordinators can aid your firm by focusing the firm's marketing attention on the client, by obtaining valuable market information on clients and other market opportunities, by interpreting technical data into a clear business message, and by assisting in developing communications from the partners, staff or firm to the client.

When selecting a coordinator for your marketing activities, identify what areas require immediate attention and focus the responsibilities of this individual in these areas. Do not try to overwhelm the marketer with so many diverse responsibilities that little can be accomplished for the firm. Define the coordinator's responsibilities to meet your firm's needs, set forth in your marketing plan. Set the marketing coordinator up to succeed.

---

## A MARKETING COORDINATOR'S EXPERIENCE
*Pamela N. Terry*
*Marketing Consultant, Houston*

Any accounting firm aggressively trying to use marketing tools effectively can benefit from having a marketing professional on staff. The size of the firm is not important; every firm is involved in marketing activities to some extent. When these activities do not yield the anticipated increased client services or new clients, the firm's partners and professionals become disenchanted with marketing. If a firm's partners want to pursue marketing and make its efforts successful, then they should consider adding a marketing professional to the staff. To identify the characteristics important to success as a marketing coordinator, we will examine my experience in that position with the Houston office of Touche Ross.

## Four Characteristics of Successful Marketing Coordinators

Once you decide to hire a marketing coordinator, you will define the characteristics of your ideal candidate. The obvious ones relate to a basic knowledge of and experience in marketing and public relations. Not so obvious are four characteristics that ensure success: (1) good listening skills; (2) knowledge of information sources; (3) effective communication skills; and (4) resourcefulness.

*Listening Skills.* The marketing coordinator must listen to everyone in the firm. Since there is no working structure for a new marketing coordinator, it is important for that individual to gather information about the accounting profession and the firm's needs from the professionals so that the right decisions for the firm are made. This is accomplished to a great extent by listening.

*Information Resource.* The professionals within a firm will depend on the marketing coordinator for all types of information. It is important to seek out information from members of the firm and other sources, and to arrange that information systematically for quick access.

*Communication Skills.* Once the information is gathered, the marketing coordinator must disseminate the information to interested people within the firm and, as appropriate, to clients, prospects, referral sources, and potential firm vendors. As an effective communicator, the coordinator will be able to educate the firm and its clients about the activities, skills and services available.

*Resourcefulness.* One of the most important characteristics of a marketing coordinator is to be resourceful. The marketing coordinator should be creative, taking a new approach to a particular situation. Having problem-solving ability to find answers and to communicate them to the appropriate client or staff is also important. By being resourceful, a marketing coordinator can implement programs that fit into your firm's operating and market structure.

A marketing coordinator should possess certain interpersonal skills to be successful in an accounting firm. By being an effective listener, being able to gather and assemble the information in an organized manner, and being resourceful, the coordinator will be more successful in communicating the importance of marketing within the firm.

## Needed: A Job Description

Firms of all sizes are hiring marketing coordinators. In fact, many offices of national firms have had coordinators for three or more years, and firms with three or four partners now have hired coordinators. Regardless of firm size, marketing coordinators are inundated with responsibilities for implementing the firm's marketing programs. These individuals can assist in the definition and implementation phases, as well as in maintaining the evaluation and control systems. If your firm is interested in being more marketable and committed to client-oriented approaches, a professional marketer can help you.

However, partners in an accounting firm do not realize the amount of responsibility a marketing coordinator can assume until that person is in the office. Without planning, it is possible to turn this position into a dumping ground because, in essence, all activities of the firm can be defined as marketing. Care should be taken to define and confine primary responsibilities until additional tasks can be added smoothly.

## MARKETING PROFESSIONALS DON'T FIT A MOLD
*Maureen Broderick*
*Price Waterhouse, San Francisco*

The selection of a marketing professional depends on the environment and working structure in which the marketing professional will function. The environment for a marketing professional is one of multiple activities—usually involving last-minute deadlines—with multiple reporting relationships. Although a marketing professional usually reports to a particular individual within a practice, in fact, a marketing professional works for all the partners. In the San Francisco office of Price Waterhouse, 35 partners each expect specific marketing activities to be accomplished in a certain time period.

The reality is that most projects tend to be a series of last-minute rushes, with the marketing professional responsible for ensuring that projects are completed on time. In addition, a marketing professional must find a place within the rigid hierarchy of the typical firm. Is she part of the "professional" staff, the "administrative" staff, or somewhere in between? What type of person can survive—and thrive—in this demanding environment?

### Surveying Professionals

Because the marketing professional's position is new to accounting firms, the information available is limited. In several international accounting firms, many local offices have hired marketing professionals, whose backgrounds and job descriptions are varied. In an effort to identify the characteristics associated with success in the demanding role of marketing professional, the participants in the first national symposium on the marketing of accounting services were surveyed to identify the requisite characteristics and skills.

The respondents to the open-ended questionnaire included marketing professionals from national, regional, and local firms. Also participating were partners and managers, many representing local accounting firms that had not yet developed marketing programs.

## Identifying Key Characteristics

The marketing professionals were asked to describe their educational background, in terms of college degree(s), and previous work experiences. In addition, they and the partner group were asked to identify the personal characteristics and skills necessary for a successful marketing professional.

*Marketing Professionals Have Diverse Backgrounds.* Marketing professionals come from a broad range of disciplines and employment backgrounds. In fact, many shifted careers dramatically when they accepted positions with accounting firms.

In terms of education, the majority had an undergraduate degree in English and/or journalism. Other undergraduate majors included psychology, accounting, business, law, marketing and art. Advanced degrees included one doctorate and master's degrees in business administration, public administration, clinical psychology, and education.

Work experience also varied. Several respondents reported marketing experience in packaged goods, insurance, real estate, nonprofits, publishing, and telecommunications. Others formerly worked in publishing, broadcasting, public relations, advertising, office administration, computer programming, and retailing.

*Nine Skills Are Necessary for Success.* Marketing professionals and partners cited communication skills, both oral and written, as necessary for success as a marketing professional in an accounting firm. The second most frequent response was knowledge of basic marketing and sales concepts.

In addition, skills in seven areas were reported.

Research

Analysis

Interpersonal, including listening

Sales/persuasiveness

Project management, including planning, administration, and budget control

Negotiation

Public relations

One participant summed up by suggesting that a marketing coordinator should possess the ability to mix the accounting professional's pragmatic approach to marketing with the marketing professional's creative, aggressive approach. Interestingly, only five respondents mentioned that marketing professionals should have a basic understanding of accounting and auditing.

***Diverse Personal Characteristics Are Important.*** Marketing professionals and partners differed slightly in their perception of the personal characteristics needed for success. On the one hand, the marketing professionals offered truly personal characteristics. First, a marketing professional should be a visionary and have stamina, patience, persistence, creativity, enthusiasm, high energy, and initiative. Further, he should have a sense of humor, "no ego," and "a very low boiling point," and should be thick-skinned and humble. Finally, marketing professionals cited business-related characteristics: good business logic and the abilities to delegate, to articulate, and to say, "No."

On the other hand, the success characteristics cited by partners related to a marketing professional's interpersonal and leadership skills. Partners mentioned that a successful marketing professional:

1. Has patience with partners
2. Inspires partners and other professionals to get involved in marketing
3. Is comfortable working as part of a team
4. Is assertive

Also mentioned were "willingness to start over" and "receptivity to change."

### Finding a Marketing Professional

Although marketing professionals have educational backgrounds in marketing, public relations, or communications, and a wide variety of employment experiences, the trend seems to indicate that individuals returning to school for advanced degrees are prime candidates for the challenge of the marketing professional's position. Knowledge of marketing fundamentals and excellent communication and interpersonal skills appear to be attributes of successful marketing professionals.

Although the results of this survey cannot be generalized, it is clear that the marketing professional's position in an accounting firm is demanding and requires a broad range of talents. However, there is no direct answer yet to the question: "How can our firm find a marketing coordinator who has these broad skills and abilities?" It is not an easy process. Some firms have used classified advertising and executive search firms. Some firms have retained public relations or advertising consultants and subsequently hired them. Other firms, including Price Waterhouse, have used graduate schools as a source. For example, as an MBA student, I consulted with the San Francisco office and created a full-time marketing position for myself.

The approach you use depends on your firm's needs and your market. The person you select is key to your firm's marketing success, so careful consideration should be given to the process. Above all, look for a person who fits well into your firm's unique environment.

---

## ☐ MARKETING RESOURCES? EVERYONE IN THE FIRM

It would be easy to conclude that establishing a marketing function in your firm would take care of all its marketing needs, but that is not the case. Rather, the implication is that the role of marketing in your firm is to make it easier for everyone in the firm to market. For example, the marketing professional may facilitate the development of an industry group's marketing plan and develop the systems for the group to check progress. However, for the plan to work, the group must own the plan; it must be theirs. Further, many of the action steps in the plan can be performed best—and frequently only—by accounting professionals. There is a limit to what marketing professionals can accomplish without the active participation of the firm's professionals.

In the client-centered firm, the service professionals understand that they are the front-line marketers because, in delivering the service, they are part of the service. Further, their frequent conversations with the client give them insights into client needs and values. As front-line marketers, they can improve their performance by working with marketing professionals.

A second implication is that your partner group must have a good understanding of your firm's needs and dynamics to determine your optimal marketing resources. If your firm needs marketing leadership because your partners can be used most profitably in client service activities, search for a person who can deliver management capability, and give that person support. If your needs are limited to proposal support, look for someone with research, writing, and administrative strengths. Selecting the right combination of marketing strengths and experience can result in successful programs. The wrong choice yields negative, frequently frustrating, results.

In the client-centered firm, marketing interacts with every other department and function to maintain the client's experiences with the firm at a consistently high quality. In the client-centered firm, everyone plays a role in marketing.

# 4

# MAKING PUBLIC RELATIONS WORK FOR YOUR FIRM

It would be difficult to find an accounting firm that does not use public relations in some way. Most accounting professionals understand its usefulness, if only in terms of publicity. Thus, a public relations firm represents a potentially valuable resource to accounting firms of all sizes.

In a smaller accounting practice with limited needs or budget constraints, a public relations firm may be the only resource available to the partner responsible for marketing. In larger firms with in-house marketing capabilities, a public relations firm may be needed to support specific aspects of the marketing plan. Whether your firm is small or large, however, if your relationship is going to be constructive and productive, you and your partners must understand the scope of public relations.

Some firms overestimate its value. These firms mistakenly equate public relations with marketing. Having heard that marketing is good and that successful firms have marketing programs, these firms engage a public relations consultant in the belief that they then will have a marketing program. In effect, the firm says to the public relations consultant, "Develop our marketing program for us."

Some time later, the consultant presents his ideas to the

partners, who consider the plans inappropriate and conclude, "The consultant doesn't understand our business." The firm ends the relationship and retains a new consultant for the same assignment without giving him any guidance. There are firms which have had three different public relations consultants in as many years. Somehow, they miss the obvious: Your firm cannot delegate responsibility for its marketing program to a public relations firm or to any other consultant.

There are other firms who expect too little from public relations. Generally, they do not understand that public relations can help them create and reinforce a firm's image. Thus, they overlook the potential that exists right in their practices, for example, news stories about the firm. Successfully increasing your firm's visibility through a public relations program relates directly to your firm's image.

To gain the benefits public relations offers as a marketing tool, your firm must manage the effort. That is true if your marketing program is run by a partner who has many competing responsibilities and no marketing staff and, thus, is dependent on an outside consultant. It is also true if you have a marketing or communications specialist on your staff.

What role does an accounting firm play in managing public relations programs? What responsibilities does the firm have? Bernard Ury, a seasoned public relations consultant who heads his own firm in Chicago, will answer these pivotal questions in the following section. Ury further describes the development of a successful public relations program in an accounting firm.

Then, Susan Fryer, the director of communications for Peat Marwick's St. Louis office, offers the firm's perspective for building a constructive working relationship with a public relations consultant. She also describes that practice's experience in building a program that works. The third section focuses on the widely used public relations tool—the seminar.

## HOW TO WORK SUCCESSFULLY WITH A PUBLIC RELATIONS CONSULTANT

*Bernard E. Ury*
*Bernard E. Ury Associates Inc., Chicago*

What is the definition of *public relations*? As a relatively new discipline, public relations is not always understood by potential users—accountants included. At times, they expect public relations people to do things and deliver results that fall outside of public relations' areas of competence. Some of the unrealistic "great expectations" we have encountered include:

Keep all bad news out of the press.

Create a public image opposite the firm's present image.

Arrange for the managing partner to appear on a major television show even if he has nothing worthwhile to say.

Guarantee that top corporate executives will attend a firm-sponsored seminar.

What can an accounting firm realistically expect of a public relations consultant?

### Defining the Public Relations Mission

The definition of public relations varies, depending on whom you ask. People have differing expectations of what results public relations can deliver. Thus, it is critical to ask the partners in your accounting firm to define the results they want to achieve and the public relations consultant's role in the process.

*Partners Set Objectives and Priorities.* For the professional service organization, the role of public relations is to build the visibility of the organization. How this is done and what the organization expects will depend on the particular organization. Further, the accounting firm must establish its own objectives and set priorities. For instance, the accounting firm's partners may decide on the following three objectives.

Increase new business by making prospects, nonclients, and the business community aware of the firm and its services.

Build business among its audit clients by making them more aware of its management advisory services, software evaluation services, or tax consulting services.

Build the morale of the firm's professional and support staff so that they are proud to be part of a firm that is constantly in the news and is well known.

The priority any accounting firm would put on these objectives depends on the individual firm. However, the point is that it is the accounting firm's responsibility to set the priorities.

***Partners Define a Firm's Image.***  The degree to which an accounting firm's visibility can be successfully increased is directly related to the firm's image. Many accountants have never answered the question, "What should our firm's image be?" They have not assessed their firm's capabilities and its past successes, nor have they considered how they want their various publics to perceive their firm. As a result, they expect a public relations consultant to tell them what their firm's image should be. This expectation is unrealistic. Only a firm's partners can determine the image appropriate for their firm. However, once that determination is made, outside public relations counsel can identify resources within the accounting firm to support the image.

***The Firm and the Public Relations Consultant Have Complementary Responsibilities.***  Public relations comprises nine general areas: public policy, image, community expectations, marketing and sales, management participation, speeches and presentations, staff relations, client relations, and government relations. In each area, the accounting firm has responsibilities that range from determining policy to serving clients well and to participating in community activities, as shown in Table 4-1. In fact, if the accounting firm does not accept responsibility in a given area, nothing will happen; the firm will be ineffectual in that public relations area.

Implicit in the table is the point that public relations cannot function without management support, including that of the managing partner. Also needed at all personnel levels are participation and cooperation, with timely responses and positive attitudes.

Table 4-1 also shows the public relations consultant's responsibilities in each area. Notice that the public relations counsel's role is to advise, to communicate, to arrange. In no instance does the public relations counsel set policy or strategy for its client. An additional responsibility of public relations counsel is to educate the accounting firm's professionals about the public relations discipline.

An effective public relations program is based on an accounting firm's policies and involvement. In fact, there are some responsibilities that the accounting firm *must* assume if a program is to be successful. Outside public relations counsel can contribute to a program's success once the accounting firm has set direction.

## Starting a Public Relations Program

Once responsibility has been recognized and accepted by the accounting firm's management, what comes first—the program or the public relations specialist?

*Develop the Program First.* In solving this chicken-or-egg dilemma, we have found that it is important to develop the program first, based on your marketing plan. You may want to hire a public relations firm as a consultant for this development project. Alternatively there may be a prospective in-house person who could assist. Next, determine what your accounting firm can spend. Then, jockey back and forth to align the program with the funds available.

Some of the tools to be considered are these.

## TABLE 4–1. PUBLIC RELATIONS RESPONSIBILITY OF AN ACCOUNTING FIRM AND ITS PUBLIC RELATIONS CONSULTANT

| Area | What Only the Accounting Firm Can Do | What a PR Consultant Can Do |
|---|---|---|
| Public policy | Determine what the accounting firm's policies should be and carry them out | Advise the accounting firm on any differences between public interest and the firm's policy, and advise on ways to close the gap |
| Image | Determine what the accounting firm's image should be | Ascertain what the accounting firm's image is, and advise on what might be done to bridge any gap between reality and desire and to sustain good image |
| Community expectations | Make and execute decisions that relate to community expectations | Determine if there are gaps between what the community expects and what the accounting firm provides; then advise on ways to remedy deficiencies |
| Marketing and sales | Determine and execute the accounting firm's marketing strategy concerning markets to be reached, pricing, packaging, advertising, and so on | Carry out, via communications, activities to support the marketing strategy |
| Management participation | Participate, such as joining and becoming active in community and trade groups | Advise on what activities—community, industry, professional—in which it would be beneficial for partners and others to participate |
| Speeches and presentations | Carry out speaking engagements and seminar or panel participation | Arrange speaking engagements, seminar participation, etc., for partners and others and help prepare them |
| Staff relations | Design and execute effective staff relations programs | Communicate policies to professional and support staff and obtain feedback for management |
| Client relations | Develop programs for good client relations; take action to remedy product and service deficiencies | Carry out communications programs with clients and prospects; determine areas of dissatisfaction; advise remedies |
| Government relations | Carry out strategies to gain government approval where needed for industry, firm progress | Estimate government reaction to proposals; prepare presentations; communicate with public for support |

Publicity

Newsletters

Brochures

Organization memberships

Reprints of articles written by accounting firm professionals

Seminars

Speaker's bureau

Any one of these tools can be used effectively within a reasonable budget.

Set realistic goals. Public relations takes time to do its work. Your firm cannot hire either a public relations consultant or an in-house public relations person and expect to see results overnight. In fact, it takes a year or more to see the results of a program.

***Designate an In-House Coordinator.*** Once your program gets started, the traffic in requests for information will escalate, especially when people in the accounting firm begin asking for public relations assistance, whether from a public relations person in the firm or from outside public relations counsel. There must be a coordinator within the firm who keeps track of requests, thus avoiding duplicate efforts and cross-filings. That person may well be your practice's marketing coordinator. If your practice does not have one, a partner or administrator could handle the overall coordination.

***Hire Press Experience for In-House.*** If your firm can afford to hire an in-house public relations person, look for a writer who has worked successfully with the press. If this person is competent, requests for assistance will be many and varied. Thus, there will be a need for coordination, as well as for setting priorities.

***Hire Public Relations Counsel for Expertise and Service.*** Your public relations objectives indicate the strengths you need in a public relations consultant. For example, if your accounting firm's name is not well known, publicity will be an important part of the public relations consultant's challenge. The first thing to do is to call the business editors in town and ask them for the names of three or four public relations consultants that they think highly of on the basis of their providing good, intelligently written copy.

Then call in the public relations consultants and ask them to give you a list of their clients. Check with the clients to find out what kind of service they receive, whether the public relations consultant's people are responsive and imaginative, and whether they keep ahead of the client in suggesting ideas and following up. The consultants themselves should be asked to identify their areas of expertise and their weak points.

In screening public relations consultants, it is also important to meet the account person who will work with your accounting firm and to spend time together to determine that there is good rapport. Friction indicates problems ahead. With the right account person, your accounting firm can build a successful public relations program.

***Use a Retainer, if Possible.*** The cost of hiring or retaining an outside public relations consultant varies from region to region. Costs will be highest in New York and San Francisco; in mid-America, they will be less. However, you can ask various public relations consultants what their charges are and then determine what you want to have them do on the basis of their rates.

If your accounting firm's marketing plan involves a public relations program, as opposed to individual events or projects, consider using a retainer, which facilitates commitment from both organizations. The retainer imposes a strict discipline on a public relations consultant to earn the money, while the accounting firm people will be responsive because they have spent that money up front and want to obtain some return for it. With the alternative—a project or an hourly basis with monthly billing—there are too many opportunities for surprises. Also, the day-to-day pressures in an accounting firm make it easy to say, "Well, I'll just put that aside. If I don't act on it, if I don't respond, I'm not going to get billed for it." Public relations programs do not flourish under these conditions.

Whether you choose a retainer or a project basis, the fee pays for time charges. In addition, you must budget for the expenses of a program or project—mimeographing releases, postage, taking editors out to lunch, photography, and the like. Public relations counsel can help you estimate these costs, which can range anywhere from 20 percent to 75 percent of the fee. Special events, like seminars, require a separate budget altogether.

## Using Publicity Effectively

Publicity involves obtaining coverage in the media—the electronic media (radio and TV) and the press—to build the image of the firm, to increase its visibility, to make its people known, to make its areas of expertise known. In obtaining publicity, we have found that it is important to begin with the basics, the events that many people consider small or insignificant. Yet, these events (e.g., announcements of people who have joined your firm, promotions to partner and other positions, and office openings or moves) do serve a purpose. Frequently overlooked is the partner who is elected to national office in a trade association, which sends out a general release with officers' names buried and, thus, unnoticed by local editors. The accounting firm's marketing coordinator can work with the trade association to obtain the information and to see that it is passed along to the local press through a news release highlighting the local partner. Remember, all media are interested primarily in news aimed at their readers' interests.

*Use the Information in Your Firm.* Out of the routine, there is a great deal of material that can be generated in an accounting firm of a service-type nature, such as tax tips. The media are always looking for material on how to save on taxes. Other topics are estate planning tips, business management pointers, and trends and observations on what is happening in the economy and what is likely to happen. There are probably several people within your accounting firm who can be the source of this information, which can be turned into news releases for your practice's target media, both local and trade.

It is up to the public relations consultant to find this material. The publicist researches the topic, usually with the accounting firm's technical gurus, and develops the story, presenting the technical information as clearly and simply as possible. During the approval process, any inaccuracies are identified and corrected, always with an eye toward the simple approach. The reason simplicity and clarity are important is that you want the release to attract an editor's attention as a newsworthy topic. A good editor does not describe a technical tax issue in technical terms. If an editor receives a release and cannot understand it, the chances are that the release will be discarded, at worst, or rewritten and possibly garbled, at best.

***Get to Know Local Press People.*** Establishing rapport and a presence with the press is also important because reporters frequently are looking for sources of commentary when a newsworthy issue rises. If they know that they can call your accounting firm and ask for a certain partner who understands the issue and is available and accessible, the press will continually come back to that person. This partner and your firm will be cited more often than other firms that do not provide this kind of service to the press.

***Hold Press Briefings.*** Press briefings are another useful vehicle for familiarizing the press with your firm. We have worked with Grant Thornton to arrange press briefings on major issues that are coming to the fore. A couple of years ago, when the latest tax bill revision was going through Congress, we alerted the press that Grant Thornton would hold a briefing to explain the major points of the bill, particularly the ramifications for the consumer and the corporate executive. That briefing was well attended by electronic and print media people because this type of information helps them do their job better. When Grant Thornton or any other accounting firm provides this information as a service to the press, the firm will be credited.

*Coordinate Advertising and Publicity.* If your accounting firm has advertising and public relations programs, they should follow common themes wherever possible. It is true that public relations and advertising differ in the degree of control your firm has over the material to be communicated. In advertising, your message appears exactly as you want it written. In publicity, it is the editor's prerogative to change your copy. However, it is possible to correlate the two. If, for example, your firm's advertising focuses on personal financial planning, publicity efforts can use the same themes. Coordination between the two areas should be handled by the accounting firm's marketing coordinator.

## What Is Success?

Success in public relations results from the interaction of four factors over a year or more:

1. The public relations program, which must be aligned with the accounting firm's marketing plan
2. Acceptance of responsibilities by both the accounting firm and the public relations consultant
3. Good coordination within the accounting firm by its marketing coordinator
4. Public relations people who are strong in the areas needed by the accounting firm and who are committed to serving your firm

---

ACCOUNTING AND PUBLIC RELATIONS FIRMS:
THE FUNDAMENTALS OF A SUCCESSFUL RELATIONSHIP
*Susan M. Fryer*
*Peat Marwick, St. Louis*

The relationship between an accounting firm and its public relations counsultant is a close, constructive one if the firm's goals are being achieved. The successful relationship will be characterized by mutual respect and teamwork—the capacity to choose and implement the activities that will reach your firm's marketing goal, regardless of who gets the credit.

This type of relationship does not develop instantaneously. It takes time for accountants to understand what public relations people do, and vice versa. In fact, when an accounting firm embarks on a public relations program for the first time, it could well take 18 to 24 months before a cohesive, results-oriented program takes shape.

There are key factors in developing a constructive relationship. Some are within the control of the accounting firm; others depend on both firms. First, an accounting firm's management must address the responsibility issue: Who is responsible for the public relations program? If the response is to hire a public relations consultant and then say, "Do it," the firm probably will never have a sound program. In-firm responsibility, covered in the next section, is critical to a program's success. Another in-firm factor is performance measurement, or keeping track of your firm's progress versus plan.

Other factors concerning the relationship depend on both organizations. Several of these factors should be considered when evaluating a public relations consultant. These factors, both tangible and intangible, are described in the section "Building a Working Relationship." In the concluding section, a real-life example shows how these factors interact when an accounting firm and a public relations consultant worked together constructively on an opportunity many firms have: the office move.

## In-Firm Responsibility

The secret to working successfully with a public relations consultant is to have someone in your accounting firm who is responsible for it. Just as a professional accounting firm cannot possibly produce results for clients without inside contact and involvement, neither can a professional public relations firm accomplish anything for its client without similar access and support. Therefore, the job of the insider is critical.

For that job, competence in communications and public relations is not enough. There are three issues that must be addressed when the insider's job description is developed and when the selection is taking place: positioning, education, and the "messiah" issue.

*Position for Success.* Every organization has a pecking order, and accounting firms, in particular, adhere to a very strict line of progression. If the person managing marketing, communications, and public relations is to be successful, that person must be carefully positioned. Unless the promotional activities are formally recognized as important, they will fall to the bottom of the list of priorities for the accounting professionals.

*Plan for Internal Marketing.* The education issue is critical because promotional activities are relatively new and unknown to most accounting professionals. Thus, the job of the insider must include internal communication so that the methods and the goals of public relations are understood and can be accepted by the firm's professionals. Here is one definition that will help your associates better understand what public relations is: A communications solution to a marketing problem.

*Public Relations Is Everyone's Job.* Third, the "messiah" issue needs to be resolved. No one person can do everything, neither the inside person nor the outside people. Good public relations is the responsibility of everyone in an organization, and the need for participation by all must be stressed from the very beginning. The more that message can be conveyed, generally by the inside person, the better.

## Measuring Progress against Goals

Once the internal responsibility is assigned, the results you want to achieve with your public relations consultant must be clearly identified and communicated throughout the firm. Do you want help on issues management? Are you looking for client publicity in addition to your own? Are you seeking community contacts? The important point to remember is that just as a consulting engagement can be many things to many different clients, so can the expectations of your firm's professionals vary widely. Thus, the public relations consultant's goals should be spelled out from the very beginning. Then, take advantage of every opportunity to help the partners and staff understand these goals.

Also, a tangible system of measurement or follow-up must be established. Clip files, broadcast logs, or computerized listings of who is on what civic or corporate board all yield useful documentation. Hold periodic review meetings with documentation to track results. Take a lesson from New York City's Mayor Ed Koch, the master of follow-up with his "How'm I doing?" Ask this question all the time. Ask it formally by market research, and ask it informally. You will find some surprises. Of course, do not ask the question if you do not want to hear the answer.

## Building a Working Relationship

To collaborate with public relations consultants, accountants should consider important aspects of the relationship itself and then incorporate these into the selection process. Basically, there are two aspects of the relationship: intangible and tangible.

The intangible aspects concern the spirit of the relationship. They can be difficult to measure, particularly in introductory meetings. Yet, it is possible to gauge rapport. Your respective teams should meet several times before final selection to verify impressions. Other intangibles to consider are creativity and problem-solving strengths. Also look for the commitment signifying a "joined" relationship in which the consultant's staff act as if your firm is their most significant client.

There are also four tangible criteria to consider. The most significant, the letter of the relationship, spells out the working relationship: fees, services provided, and responsibilities. A public relations firm should demonstrate qualifications to support your firm's marketing needs with appropriate experience and qualified personnel, including writers and freelancers. Ask the president of the public relations firm for a written proposal covering these points; evaluate each point in relation to your firm's needs and priorities.

*Is There Rapport?* How well do we fit with each other's style of doing business? Are we on the same wavelength? Are we comfortable and confident in each other's presence? Do we share a sense of humor? Rapport is a subtle quality that is sometimes easier to recognize by its absence. Its dictionary meaning is harmony or agreement, and it is usually described with, "We're in sync," or "We're on the same wavelength." When rapport exists, people feel comfortable with each other, able to trust and believe in each other. Rapport is essential in any successful professional relationship.

*Look for Evidence of Creativity.* Another intangible that is necessary for a productive relationship is creativity. One way to release creative thoughts is brainstorming, an approach we use at Peat Marwick in St. Louis with our consultant, Fleischman-Hillard, Inc. When we brainstorm, anything is possible. All kinds of crazy ideas are discussed, increasing our sense of the possible. In the brainstorming process, we also reinforce each other's enthusiasm for our mutual goals and objectives.

*Can They Solve Problems?* Cooking up publicity gimmicks and being mentioned in the newspaper are not the focal points of a successful public relations program. Most accounting firms have real problems (or opportunities, as we prefer to call them). Creative public relations people can help to resolve some of these concerns and to develop realistic solutions.

What we like to do is come up with a problem, which is fairly easy, and then present it to our consultant and say, "What do you think we ought to do about this? Come back to us in a few days with your ideas." This is also a good technique to use in evaluating candidates. Further, the response is an invaluable service from the public relations consultant you select, and their people also have more invested in those particular solutions. We have found that the input from an objective, outside source familiar with many public relations programs can be more effective than some of the suggestions from people within our firm.

*Are They Committed to Your Firm?* Another intangible indicating the spirit of the relationship is joined, not joint, responsibil-

ity. A public relations consultant does not have the final responsibility; the proverbial buck stops inside, not out. Ideally,
however, the public relations staff should approach each project
as if they were responsible and as if the accounting firm were
their only client.

A public relations consultant must have persistence to follow
through with the details an effective public relations program
requires. For example, contrary to what many people think,
you do not write a news release, send it to an editor, and wait
for an article, as written in the release, to appear in the paper.
There are decisions to be made about what is newsworthy and
what is appropriate for the media. Fact-gathering, writing,
rewriting, and obtaining approvals make the development of a
news release a lengthy process. Follow-up with media people
also takes time and discipline. The personal follow-up call is
absolutely essential. If an editor is interested, more calls follow
to other people in your firm who can expand on the material.
Persistence and discipline make these detail-heavy activities
yield important publicity results for your firm.

A real-life example will illustrate one public relations consultant's commitment. Every year the St. Louis office of Peat
Marwick conducts a major seminar for its banking clients, and
there is a lot to do. The partners select the themes and the
speakers. The marketing staff coordinates the handout materials, as well as audiovisual requirements and other arrangements. Fleischman-Hillard, outside counsel, sends out the news
advisory based on the seminar. At the seminar, the results of
an annual survey are announced, which generates a lot of media interest. Thus, it is necessary that a communications professional be available throughout the day to help reporters arriving at different times obtain information. This past year we
held several events on the same day, which caused a coverage
problem. Fleischman-Hillard quickly recognized the situation's
importance and made professional staff available to cover these
events with, and for, us. This quality of going beyond what is
expected ultimately makes a relationship truly successful.

***Align Public Relations Expertise with Firm Goals.*** Select a public
relations consultant who has experience and expertise consis-

tent with your practice's marketing plan. For instance, if your firm has an agribusiness practice, engage a public relations consultant who is knowledgeable about that industry and familiar with its trade publications. If you want assistance in placing your people in community organizations, find a consultant who has solid connections.

*Review Communications Support.* Accounting firms produce a great deal of technical information. Public relations people frequently must parlay that information into the general public pool of information. That process may require the assistance of good writers, so you should review examples of work they have done for other clients.

*Identify Freelance Resources.* When you are evaluating a public relations consultant, look not only for the talents that they have within, but also for their ability to bring in other resources when needed. When your firm has a major event, you should not hear, "We've got six clients, and they're all having something today. We can't help you." A good firm has a roster of freelancers who can help to get the job done.

*Define the Working Relationship in Writing.* The letter of the relationship is the most tangible aspect of your firm's relationship with a public relations firm. It is critical to spell out what the agreed-on working relationship is (e.g., a retainer or a project basis). The billing agreements need to be understood by as many people as possible, not just your internal marketing person and the head of the public relations firm. For example, your firm's controller should know exactly what the billing agreements are, as should partners and others who have an interest. If people clearly understand what you have contracted for, what you have agreed to pay, and what results you expect, you will have fewer problems.

Should your firm hire a public relations consultant for specific projects or on a retainer? Most insiders who have used a retainer find that this approach works successfully because there is a two-way commitment. The public relations consultant has the interest and takes the time to do all the homework and research; this deep commitment is not possible on a "per project" basis. In addition, when you know that your firm is paying for services, you will have a continuing interest in the activities and ensure that your firm is taking advantage of the services.

With regard to out-of-pocket expenses for specific projects, approval should be obtained in advance. The partner who decides to use rear-screen projection at the last minute should approve that expenditure before arrangements are made. For individual production items (e.g., a brochure or a set of slides), ask for itemized bills. In the St. Louis market, there is a standard 15 percent markup for these types of services. Our procedure is to arrange for services in advance—the newswire, graphics, or opinion research—and to obtain separate billing for each service.

Another item in the letter that is helpful both internally and for outside counsel is our publicity and special events schedule. This month-by-month listing of planned publicity and special events is based on our office's annual plan, which, in turn, reflects Peat Marwick's national plan. We do update the office plan monthly, at least, but we are not locked in. The schedule provides a focus, a reference point. Circulated throughout the firm, the schedule is a tickler for many people. We recognize, though, that the schedule must be flexible if it is to work, and we do make changes frequently.

A well-developed letter of agreement provides direction for the working relationship. Misunderstandings and arguments over billings and services obstruct the momentum your respective organizations are building.

## Cooperation Counts

Public relations people bring an objective problem-solving perspective to business situations faced by accountants and, thus, can be very helpful. The following example shows how a public relations consultant and accountants can work together constructively toward an accounting firm's marketing goals.

Your firm is moving to new quarters, an exciting event for

your firm, but hardly worthy of a feature in the business section of your local newspaper. A public relations consultant can be very helpful in a brainstorming session to find out what is unique about your move and what people would be interested in that unique point. These questions must be addressed if you are going to have media coverage. When the St. Louis office of Peat Marwick moved, we obtained coverage in major local media by focusing on the office's newly assembled collection of paintings and photographs by local artists.

For this move, our public relations consultant did something especially important in suggesting that we appoint an in-house committee to work on this project, to take responsibility for all the arrangements. The effect was to give many Peat Marwick people an opportunity to expand their knowledge about the firm and St. Louis. They were enthusiastic and supportive. At the same time, we could take advantage of the consultant's expertise. Much of the success of that event could be attributed to the communication and support between the two firms.

A public relations consultant can be especially helpful for these special events because of the sheer volume of additional work that is not routine in most accounting firms. We do not routinely send out formal invitations with RSVPs, three enclosures, a piece of artwork, and a plastic champagne glass with the firm's name on it—and all in Peat Marwick's colors. This is not the usual mode of doing business. A public relations consultant can introduce you to suppliers—florists, magicians, whomever you need for this event.

However, the most important point in working successfully with a public relations consultant is to have someone in the firm responsible for the public relations program. This person is key to developing the relationship that yields success.

## ☐ SUCCESS IN PUBLIC RELATIONS

Both Ury and Fryer emphasized several points underlying successful public relations programs.

Your firm sets policy and direction for a public relations program.

Your firm must have a marketing plan to provide the direction.

Someone inside the firm must have ongoing responsibility for coordinating public relations activities.

In the process of selecting a public relations firm, look for rapport, industry credentials, and service quality.

Hire a consultant on retainer, if possible, to gain commitment from the consultant and the firm.

There is an unexpected bonus in working with a public relations consultant—or a market research organization, an advertising agency, or other marketing consultant. When your firm engages one of these consultants who will gain an intimate knowledge of your firm, your firm becomes its client. The experiences you have as a client give you valuable insights into a service delivery system somewhat similar to an accounting firm's. For example, both organizations deal in intangibles. Also, both bill for time spent. You will find yourself saying, "Oh, this is what our clients go through."

One public relations activity many firms agree is useful is the seminar. Financial planning, accounting issues, new tax legislation are only a few of the seminar topics possible. Some seminars are huge successes, attracting many more attendees than anyone in the sponsoring firm imagined. Other firms go through the same steps and draw only five or six people. What happened to cause so many yawns? Pamela N. Terry, who heads her own consulting practice, describes the seminar planning process that results in success, new business.

---

## SEMINAR SAVVY WITH STYLE
*Pamela N. Terry*
*Marketing Consultant, Houston*

When Congress passes new tax legislation or the Small Business Administration announces a new program to help entrepreneurs manage their companies better, how can your firm let clients and prospects know that your professionals not only understand the topic, but also can help clients benefit from the information? One particularly effective vehicle could be a seminar—if it is planned well, if the topic and speakers are interesting and entertaining, and if the firm's professionals follow up.

## What Is the Purpose?

Before any planning is done, it is important to ask, "Why should the firm sponsor this seminar?" Another firm or office may have had great success with a particular seminar topic, but that does not mean this event fits into your practice's marketing plan. From the start, seminar planners must understand their goals. No matter what you want to achieve, you have two basic purposes. The primary purpose is to create an image about your accounting firm. The secondary purpose is to educate, to inform.

*Identify the Image to Be Projected.* In using a seminar to help create an image, consider what you want to communicate to your audience. Certainly you want to create an image that is first-class and professional. Additionally, you may want to let your market know that your firm's professionals are knowledgeable in a certain area—issues in an industry, perhaps, or new tax legislation. You may want people to know that your firm's professionals are friendly, approachable people. Your seminar should be consistent with the image your partners want to communicate.

*Relate Every Detail to the Purpose.* When you have a clear grasp of the image you want to project, relate everything about the seminar to that goal. Everyone working on the seminar, regardless of the person's role, should know the purpose. That includes the secretary who works on the mailing list and the switchboard operator who takes calls. Behind-the-scenes administrators can be more effective when they understand the purpose of the seminar and the kind of image the firm wants to project.

A seminar makes a statement about your firm. The clarity of that statement depends on how well everyone understands the seminar's purpose. Therefore, define the image to be projected and relate all details to that image.

## Upbeat Topics and Speakers

The topic and speakers you choose are important not only in creating an image, but also in attracting people to attend. Most potential attendees are busy people, and your seminar, subject, and speakers must catch their attention.

***Relate Your Topic to Your Audience's Needs.*** If your topic appeals to your audience's needs, people will attend. For example, two partners in your firm may know a lot about financing. You must establish that topic's relevance to your audience. Many of your clients and prospects may be weighing alternatives to help meet growth objectives, and financing may be one alternative. You then could relate financing to growth with an upbeat, fresh title like: "Financing: The Yellow Brick Road to Growth." Most people associate the yellow brick road with gold and success. Thus, if they are considering growth vehicles, they might find this topic attractive. Your choice of topic is important because it is one of the first considerations when a person decides whether or not to attend.

***Find the Most Impressive Speakers Possible.*** While seminar planners have almost complete control over the topic, they have less control over the quality of the presenters in terms of their speaking abilities. Unless you have heard someone speak, you really cannot be sure how a speaker will be received. At a minimum, find speakers who are knowledgeable about a subject. The presentation should be informative, at least, and, at most, entertaining, too.

When your firm's professionals are the speakers, they can rehearse and polish their presentations. However, when your principal speaker is someone known only by reputation, you are running a risk. Since this person's reputation will draw an audience, you might have the speaker attend a reception following the seminar so that people can speak with him or her informally. The chances are good that your audience will enjoy the personal interchange even if the formal presentation is less than dynamic. The overall impression will then be positive.

## Details, Details, Details

A seminar planner who remains sane probably has found or developed a set of checklists covering the hundreds of details involved. For example, if a hotel is the seminar site, you will want to check the room's location, size, acoustics, etc. Another checklist is a schedule of key activities related to the event, such as mailing the invitations, ordering audio-visual equipment, and contacting media representatives. [One checklist used at one Big Eight firm appears in the Appendix.]

Three areas in which attention to detail pays off are invitations, mailing lists, and visuals and handouts. The payoff comes, respectively, when an invitation is read, when the right person is invited, and when visuals and other materials complement the presentation.

*Design Inviting Invitations.* Invitations are assumed to be read by the recipient. Sometimes that is true, sometimes not. In planning your seminar, find the invitation that is most likely to be read. Basically there are three types of invitation: personal letters, flyers, and one-of-a-kind invitations. Each has its advantages, if well thought out.

Personal letters are terrific—if the reader concludes that a letter is personal. With the widespread use of word processing, many personal letters are really form letters, and the recipient knows that. What happens to the letter? It is thrown away. You are more likely to have a personal letter read if the recipient knows the person signing the letter. That signature is what makes a personal letter "personal."

Flyers can be used effectively if they are professionally designed and have a distinctive look. Your flyer must stand out. The drawback is that many flyers do not get read. Secretaries frequently screen mail for business executives, who have left instructions to give low or no priority to flyers. If you are mailing to 1000 or more people, the flyer may be the best invitation, but its success depends on a well-conceived design developed by professionals from an advertising or graphics agency.

The third type of invitation guarantees a review because it is designed to be different. An unconventional invitation draws attention and says that your firm is imaginative and creative. This invitation must relate to your purpose. In the Houston office of Touche Ross, we used this type successfully, although the event was not a seminar. However, it is a good example. The office supports a training program for young gymnasts, some of whom are world-class competitors. As part of the office's support, we sponsored a send-off reception for two then-Olympic contenders who trained in Houston, Julianne McNamara and Mary Lou Retton. We sent each invitee a poster of the two girls in a gymnastic pose, with a tasteful tagline mentioning Touche Ross Houston. Suitable for framing, the poster was mailed in a tube accompanied by an invitation to the gala, with mention of the Olympics and the firm's support. We had a very high response with this invitation; 50 percent of those invited attended.

A firm's professionals find this special invitation appealing, too. In fact, once the number of invitations is estimated, it probably should be increased by 50 percent or more to allow for the mailing list additions people want to make when they see the special invitation. This one-of-a-kind invitation requires special help, perhaps from a public relations firm, a graphics artist, or an advertising agency. We used an advertising agency to assist with the poster.

In summary, a firm probably should use the personal letter most frequently because it can be controlled within the firm and it is economical. For smaller seminars, particularly those in a series designed for clients and a selected group of prospects, the personal letter is ideal. The flyer and the unique invitations do require professional assistance and are expensive.

However, for that special event, the one-of-a-kind invitation is read and remembered.

*Fine-Tune Mailing Lists.* The best mailing list an accounting firm can have is right there in the firm: clients, alumni, referral sources, the press, academicians, and cultural leaders. A well-organized, accurate list saves a great deal of time and effort for seminar planners. If your firm does not have a mailing list computerized, it is worth the effort and saves wheel reinvention.

Whether you use a word processing system or a microcomputer, organize the list so that you can sort it on key variables: the firm representative, industry, zip code, title, etc. Thus, if your firm plans a seminar for controllers, you can extract a mailing list by that title. An additional sort by firm representative will tell you the person who should sign the invitation. By having this list computerized, you have a way to track invitations to individuals, too. Mailing lists need frequent monitoring to maintain accuracy.

There are other sources of mailing lists. Dun & Bradstreet and Standard & Poor's are only two of a large number of database sources. Many communities have a directory of corporations, perhaps through the chamber of commerce or a trade association. If you cosponsor an event with another organization (e.g., a university), that organization may have a mailing list which your firm could access. When you evaluate outside mailing lists, check the recency of update.

*Develop Quality Visuals and Handouts.* The parts of the seminar controlled by your firm's speakers should be supported by high-quality visual aids and handouts. Relate these to the purpose of your seminar, too.

Many accountants and consultants are beginning to understand how to use slides and other visual aids to complement their presentations. Instead of cramming as much material as possible onto the slide and causing the audience to squint at a visual, slide copy should be simple and concise. A visual aid

highlights and emphasizes key points. It also can break monot-
ony; cartoon-type drawings can illustrate a point, for example.

Handouts serve another purpose: to provide information that
is too detailed to present orally or that allows attendees to
study a topic in more depth than a presentation allows. A well-
organized handout should relate to the purpose of your seminar. If your purpose is to portray your firm's professionals as
knowledgeable about issues in an industry, present the speakers' biographies with an emphasis on their industry experience
and involvement. Also include a copy of your firm's newsletter
featuring an article oriented toward the industry.

Visual aids and handouts deserve high priority in planning
because they are, by definition, visible. The care with which
they are prepared sends a message to the audience about your
firm's concern for quality.

When a seminar runs smoothly, a lot of planning preceded
that event. Successful implementation involves close attention
to detail, particularly in those areas that are most apparent to
your target audience. Understanding the purpose of the seminar is key, and checklists and experience also help a great deal.

## Follow-Up: Vital to Seminar Success

Good seminar planning involves follow-up planning.[1] Why? It
is important to plan the follow-up early if only because other
competing activities become priority items after a seminar has
taken place. Also, it is possible to incorporate follow-up activities into the seminar itself if they are planned in advance.

*Provide for Audience Participation.* Create opportunities for dialogue between attendees and your firm's professionals. Break-
out sessions can be ideal for developing relationships. Someone
from your firm should take notes so that a firm representative
can follow up with a letter or telephone call to say: "At our
seminar, you raised a question about (subject), and I think I
can give you the information you need." This type of follow-up
is much easier for most people than a cold call.

*Leave Some Questions Unanswered.* Many of the seminar topics appropriate to accounting firms are technical in nature. Usually the speakers are especially knowledgeable and could respond to a question with a very lengthy, and sometimes very boring, explanation. The moderator should acknowledge that the question involves a technical explanation and provide a sign-up sheet for people who would like more information. Subsequently someone from the firm can send appropriate literature and call personally.

*Use an Evaluation Form.* Most people who attend seminars are willing to provide evaluative feedback. A summary of the results, with an appropriate cover letter, could be sent to the participants, as well as to people who registered but could not attend. The cover letter could mention suggested topics for future seminars and the firm's plans to hold these sessions.

*Conduct a Telephone Follow-Up.* Partners and managers who participate in a seminar can call attendees to inquire about their thoughts and reactions. An opening line might be: "Hello, Sam (or Mr. Brown). This is Ed Duncan with Rogers and Duncan. I'm calling to thank you for attending our seminar on financing and to find out if the program provided the information you need."

You also could solicit suggestions for future programs and answer questions. The attendee might not have any penetrating insights about the seminar, but may want to talk about a problem that an accountant could help to resolve. The possibilities are numerous once the contact is made.

For most seminars, follow-up is the weakest part, yet it is critical to your firm's purpose of obtaining business. The best follow-up procedures are based on personal interactions, such as discussion during or after the seminar. The seminar provides the opportunity to start the discussion. Follow-up keeps the discussion going.

## Conclusion

Seminars can be an effective part of a marketing program. Your purpose in holding the seminar must be clear to all the firm's participants, so that all the related activities are focused toward that purpose. Probably no one has ever counted the details associated with even the simplest breakfast seminar, but there must be at least 1000. The planner's success in handling these details is directly related to the success of the program itself. The longer-term benefits of the seminar to an accounting firm depend on the follow-up process.

## ☐ WHERE DOES THE BUCK STOP?

Making public relations work for your firm requires continual planning and evaluation for two very important reasons. First, you want to ensure that the public relations programs and activities your firm supports are consistent with and integral to your firm's marketing plan. Second, you want to make sure that you and your partners obtain the results you want from the activities, whether they are seminars, alumni events, or trade association programs.[2]

To manage this process effectively, your firm's marketing partner or director should meet regularly, perhaps monthly, with the public relations consultant to establish a detail work plan for the coming time period and to agree on the budget. Public relations people, in the course of a month, can think of many ways to help your firm, and they, like you, are under pressure to be billable. Some of their ideas will directly support your firm's plans; others, while good ideas, will not. You want to be sure that the firm's resources are used on the supporting ideas. Thus, you need a work plan and budget to define the scope of activities and to evaluate performance and progress. In this way, you will manage the process of increasing and improving your firm's visibility in its markets. Moreover, your firm will have a constructive working relationship with its public relations consultant.

# ☐ NOTES

1. See Wade Seal's comments in "Seminar Tips," *CPA Marketing Report* (April 1984): 7.
2. For expanded discussions of other public relations and promotional activities, see Robert W. Denney, *Marketing Accounting Services* (New York: Van Nostrand Reinhold Company, 1983) and Richard A. Connor, Jr., and Jeffrey P. Davidson, *Marketing Your Consulting and Professional Services* (New York: Wiley, 1985), as well as such industry-oriented publications as *CPA Marketing Report* and *The Practical Accountant.*

# 5

# ADVERTISING
# YIELDS RESULTS . . .
# IF YOU DO IT RIGHT

Of all the promotional tools, advertising is neither widely accepted nor widely used by accounting firms. The reasons are varied. Some people believe that it is too costly for the results achieved; others say that advertising is unprofessional.[1] These arguments were countered in two studies of corporate financial officers' views of advertising by accounting firms.[2] The findings suggested that:

1. Advertisements should focus on industry credentials.
2. Advertisements should cite ways in which a potential client would be helped by specific services.
3. Industry trade journals and other publications aimed at financial executives are good vehicles in which to place advertisements.

What, then, is standing in the way? The most significant reason is that most professionals have little, if any, understanding of the advertising discipline.

The potential benefits to an accounting firm which advertises are many, including:

1. Increased awareness of the firm in general or of the specific services it offers
2. A sense of pride among clients and professionals
3. Preparation of the prospective client for a meeting with the firm's professionals
4. A source of leads.

Your firm must decide if advertising meets its needs. To make this decision knowledgeably requires an understanding of advertising—what it can and cannot achieve for your firm. Also, advertising agencies must recognize that the needs of professional service firms differ significantly from those of the agencies' largest clients, usually product-oriented companies.

These two points are the focus of this chapter. First, Michael Dunleavy, director of marketing development with KMG Main Hurdman, explains the accounting firm's point of view on the firm-agency relationship, which is the foundation of any advertising program. Then, Robert Killian, a vice president with Bozell, Jacobs, Kenyon & Eckhardt, describes the agency perspective. "Strange Bedfellows: How to Work Successfully with an Advertising Agency" deals not only with the firm-agency relationship, but with principles of good advertising as well.

## ACCOUNTING FIRMS AND ADVERTISING AGENCIES CAN WORK TOGETHER IF . . .
*Michael F. Dunleavy*
*KMG Main Hurdman*

Since the profession's ban on advertising was lifted, advertising by accounting firms has not progressed very far. To describe it kindly, our campaigns are far from dramatic. Part of the reason is that neither accountants nor advertising account executives have successfully figured out how to use this powerful communication tool for professional service organizations. One real-life case study will make this clear.

Several years ago, the partner in charge of a major firm's marketing department convinced the firm's chairman that the firm must advertise to protect its client base from the lures of the advertising campaigns the firm's competitors would undoubtedly undertake. The chairman agreed to proceed, with two conditions: The agency must be one of the Top 20; and no accounting firm could have been among the agency's clients during the immediate past five years.

The easy part was identifying the Top 20. Marketing staff then spent three months looking at every single client each agency had during the previous five years. Some of the staff were assigned to this project full time, a substantial investment. The search yielded three candidates which had never been tainted by even talking with another accounting firm. They were "pure," so to speak.

At this point, the chairman reviewed the results. He selected one agency and called its chairman to tell him that it was only appropriate that one of the major accounting firms should engage one of the top advertising agencies. He then invited the agency chairman to a series of discussions about the relationship the two firms would have and the kinds of advertising programs that would be developed.

At the end of the fourth discussion, the agency chairman said, "Well, I don't know what your program will look like, but it will cost your firm $3 or 4 million dollars to start." This number seemed a bit high to the accounting firm chairman.*

However, the chairman really believed that advertising was the right vehicle, so he replied, "Fine. I don't know what the ac-

*Editors' note. This number may seem high to you, too. However, many professional service firms run successful advertising campaigns with relatively small budgets. The points discussed here apply to any successful campaign, small or large.*

tual number will be, but let's get started. Do what you have to do!"

The project started with the assignment of the advertising agency's account executive, who immediately met with the chairman and the marketing partner in charge. They told the account executive to move right ahead, but with certain restrictions: Agency people could not speak with any clients or conduct any research outside the firm; they could not tell anyone outside the agency that the accounting firm was now a client; and they could work only with six to ten senior partners and managers of the firm who understood the message that should be communicated and who knew how the agency should present the firm's story.

With all these restrictions, the agency team did an excellent job. They developed a campaign that would hold up well today. Even a media plan was developed. All that appeared to be needed was approval from the firm. The account executive presented the campaign to the firm chairman, who responded, "This is just great. Now we've got something we can take to our executive committee."

At the next executive committee meeting, the agency team presented their campaign to the firm's ten senior partners, who pulled out their lead pencils and started to make changes—adjusting a phrase here, adding a sentence there. Three years later, the partners were still making changes.

This example points out several areas that worked against the firm's success. Knowing what you want to accomplish—what image you want to communicate—is important, of course. But it is more important to recognize that, in the development of advertising, you are building a constructive relationship with the agency team.

The sections that follow focus on four key areas.

How to select an advertising agency

Building a strong working relationship

Direct mail

The advantages of public relations versus advertising

## Four Rules of Thumb:
## Engaging the Right Agency

There are four main considerations in hiring an advertising agency: size, the consultative function, the fee arrangement, and the client mix.

*Find an Agency Your Own Size.* Your agency should be comparable to your accounting firm in size. No accounting firm—even the very largest—will be spending enough money in the near term to be significant to one of the Top 20 advertising agencies. This point is not intended to be negative. Indeed, several major firms have major advertising agencies, but more because they think they should than because their advertising needs are great. In actuality, the amount of work these agencies perform for the international firms is miniscule.

*Search for a Consultant.* One of the best qualities your advertising account executive has is perspective. Agency people have an amazing perspective that is broad and eclectic. They have had different business experiences from anyone in accounting. When a marketer has no one in-house with whom to discuss marketing problems and opportunities, this consultative role can be particularly helpful.

*Discuss Fees.* Like accounting firms, advertising agencies sell time. Their people spend time doing research and creating copy and art. Projects are billed on a time-plus-expenses basis. When agency people say they are doing great creative work, accountants are likely to respond, "What am I getting for my money? Give me something on paper that I can see and touch." What we in accounting firms do not realize is that advertising agencies do to us exactly what we do to our clients.

If your firm engages an agency for media placement, your account executive should tell you the costs of various alternatives. Agencies receive a percentage, usually 15 percent, of the placement fee, and the agency fee comes off the top. In the case described above, the accounting firm did not know about the percentage for placement; it would have amounted to $600,000. Furthermore, should you decide not to run the advertisements, as the firm in the example did, your firm will be billed; the agency in the example sent a bill for about $250,000, and the firm's marketing people went into shock. Does your firm have an alternative? Some firms are using the retainer method with success.

***Hire an Agency on Retainer, Not on Media Placement.*** This point is critical. Working with a retainer allows you to pick up the telephone and say, "Let's have lunch. I've got an idea I need your input on," or "This opportunity has come up. Can you come by for an hour or so this afternoon to discuss it?" This arrangement is not expensive if you use it well. In addition, you are not worrying about a series of charges for small projects. An added benefit is that your firm's partners can call the agency informally and discuss questions or ideas they have. Partners like this service, and they think it is free. Frequent calls would not be part of a fee-for-work arrangement.

How does a retainer work? You pay the agency a flat fee per month. Every quarter you and the account executive jointly evaluate the agency's work. Has the agency team earned that fee? Should it have been more? You will not have hard data, but you will be able to answer some key questions: "Have I talked to them a lot?" "Have I spent a lot of time with them?" "Have they called me with new ideas?" The answers will give you a good indication of the agency's performance.

***Look for a Good Client Mix.*** Is the agency attracting new exciting clients fairly regularly? Does the agency have a stable client base of organizations whose advertisements are widely seen and which encourage the agency to be creative? If the answer to these questions is, "Yes," the agency probably has good creative people. You then will have better creative people assigned to your account—people with better understanding of your needs and better abilities to communicate your firm's message to its markets. The creative shop, which generates the ideas, is key to the success of your firm's advertising.

## The Firm-Agency Relationship: Two Key Elements

Most professionals are unsophisticated about the advertising process, and most advertising people do not know this. As a result, relationships can be strained as each side has different expectations of the other. If they are going to work together successfully, accountants must learn that advertising is a discipline, and advertising people have a responsibility to educate accountants about the process.

*Advertising People Have a Discipline.* As a discipline, advertising has certain steps that the agency personnel and the advertiser must follow. There is a reason for conducting research before embarking on an advertising project. There is a step for formulating the research goals and writing them down. It is much easier to be a good client if one understands the process.

Ask your agency's account executive to explain the process associated with any project or campaign undertaken. When planning a campaign, request time estimates. When an estimate for a phase seems long, find out the reasons, as this phase probably is one you do not understand completely. The details will give you a clearer understanding of the agency's activities.

*Advertising People Must Teach Accountants.* Advertising people are very bright; they understand markets; they know how to sell consumer goods very well. Part of their success comes from working with marketers of consumer goods, who are very knowledgeable about the benefits of advertising and how to use an agency effectively. Those few advertising people who have ventured into services have attempted to transfer their discipline directly from consumer goods. In banking, there has been some success; for example, a number of banks have waged successful campaigns to attract IRA business.

However, very few advertising people have worked with professional services firms, to which formal marketing is so new. As a result, most advertising people do not realize that they are dealing with unsophisticated buyers. Few accountants understand how the advertising business runs, how advertising is developed, or what research really means and why it is important.

Advertising people must teach professionals how to work with them. It must be frustrating to come into an accounting firm and find that there are eight or 440 reviewers, that decisions are made by committee, and that the information available is limited. If the level of sophistication in professional firms is going to rise, advertising account executives must take the initiative to educate accountants and other professionals.

The reality is that accountants must build a relationship with advertising people because they bring skills that accounting firms need to pursue markets. However, the initiative will have to come from the advertising account executives.

## Who Are the Key Players?

The relationship between an accounting firm and its advertising agency hinges on two key people: a partner with decision-making power and the advertising account executive. Their roles and responsibilities differ, but they influence each other's activities a great deal.

*A Partner Must Be Responsible for Advertising.* In most firms, the decision to advertise is a major one and a significant expense. It is very important that the firm's internal processes be developed to move an advertising project forward. Decisions must be made—frequently on short notice. The person responsible for the firm's activities must have a partner's power and credibility. Although a firm's marketing director or marketing coordinator certainly can play a major role, the overall responsibility must reside with a partner.

That partner should be designated early in the process. If the partner is involved when the problem is set forth and the strategy is developed, he will bring that knowledge to the review of the agency's execution. The partner becomes the project's parent, who makes the firm's internal processes work to get the project completed.

One of the important functions the partner can perform is to help the advertising account executive understand the firm and its business. When agency people do not have access to this information, an advertisement will usually be rejected by the firm because "It's not what we want." On the fifth or sixth iteration, when junior staff are assigned to the project, the advertisement will be "just what we had in mind." Keeping the agency's best people uninformed stunts creativity. The partner can keep communication open between the two organizations.

*A Good Advertising Executive Is a Consultant.* The advertising account executive deals with a client's advertising program on a day-to-day basis. If you are directing your firm's advertising program, your account executive must be someone you like, trust, and respect; someone with whom you can speak openly and directly; someone you would invite to your home for dinner. The reality is that the account executive is key to all the activities that happen, making sure that the best people are assigned, that work is turned around quickly, that questions are answered promptly. With the right account executive, an accounting firm will obtain the most value for its investment.

To be effective, the agency's account executive must understand your firm: Is the firm profitable? Who are its clients, and why did they select the firm? What are the firm's strengths and weaknesses? An account executive cannot do a good job without knowing this information. With an understanding of your organization, an account executive who is on retainer can be invaluable in a number of areas, including new service development, industry programs, public relations, and office marketing programs.

To illustrate, when KMG Main Hurdman effected a major regional merger on the West Coast, many people had different thoughts about how this merger with John Forbes & Co. should be announced. There were advocates for an advertisement in the *Wall Street Journal*; others wanted regional advertising. People had different ideas about the message itself. Agreement seemed impossible. We explained the problem to our account executive, who developed an approach acceptable to the two key decision makers. The concept was simple. The advertisement would feature a high-quality photograph of a handshake between two partners representing the two firms. The account executive's objectivity and perspective not only moved the announcement forward, but also helped to solidify the working relationship between the two merged firms. There was an added benefit: Several accountants noted that advertising people can help the profession.

The success of an advertising program depends strongly on two people. The designated partner can deliver support and action within the accounting firm. For the agency side, the account executive not only oversees the agency's work, but also can act as a consulting resource to the accounting firm.

## Direct Mail: A Good Investment

Direct mail is a good vehicle for accounting firms because they have identifiable, finite market segments for which they provide services. Individual companies in these segments can be contacted with a tailored letter and other material. A firm's advertising agency can be very helpful in developing the contents. The campaign, when well executed, involves more than writing a letter; front-end research and follow-up are key aspects of the campaign, which has high costs but offers high returns.

*Develop Your Own List.* Many accountants think that direct response involves writing a letter, printing it on good stock, mailing it to target companies, and waiting for the telephone to ring. The companies' names and addresses are purchased from a direct list house. This program sounds terrific because it involves so little work and costs relatively little; the list, printing, and postage are the major expenses.

These accountants do not realize that most mailing lists are three years old, at a minimum; many are five or seven years old. A list vendor should be able to supply this information, and the purchaser should add two years to the estimate. During a three-, five-, or seven-year period, titles change, names change, and locations change. The naive direct response planner could just as well be aiming a campaign toward "Dear Occupant."

An accounting professional cannot afford to direct a mailing to "John Jones, Treasurer" in the hope that he still holds that position. If your target is to perceive the firm's professionals as knowledgeable and well informed, the letter should begin with the target's correct name, title, and address. Lists must be cleaned up.

How do you clean up a list? An example will clarify the process. KMG Main Hurdman targeted a specific service—high-priced—to treasurers of companies within a certain sales range and within a specific geographic market. We started out with a list of 200 treasurers. Our agency provided research assistance to enhance the information by telephone interviews. When we mailed our letter, which was written by the agency, we knew we had the right names, titles, and addresses, although we had only 35 individuals remaining on the list. A list always shrinks, by the way.

*Direct Mail Works.* Follow-up is critical to a campaign's success, and you must plan for the next stage: the call. In our example, we obtained an 80 percent response rate, meaning that our professionals actually sat in the offices of 80 percent of the treasurers to whom we sent letters. Of the 28 with whom we spoke, seven purchased the service, at $14,000 to $15,000 per engagement.

*Direct Mail Pays Off.* Our campaign more than paid for itself. This campaign cost our firm about $35,000, or $1,000 per contact. With new business totaling about $100,000, our return was 3:1. Included in the costs were a letter and a special small brochure, along with the list-cleaning process, printing, and mailing. The mailing list cleanup was, by far, the most expensive part of the campaign. On a per-name basis, cleaning up can cost up to $400. There is no substitute for the careful research needed to identify the people who are the purchasers of your firm's services.

Direct mail is the only method which allows a firm to track its results so carefully. If a campaign is conducted with quality, it will convey an image of quality and, thus, predispose a prospective client to buy services. An advertising agency can assist with the letter and other materials to be mailed, as well as in developing the procedures for cleaning up the list and conducting the cleanup. Direct mail can, and should, pay for itself.

## Advertising or Public Relations?

If you are debating whether to communicate through advertising or public relations campaigns, you have two major criteria on which to compare them: time and costs. Two additional considerations are contacts and office dispersion.

*Public Relations Works Today.* Public relations is now, today. A decision to advertise, however, represents a commitment to the longer term. Your firm's marketing plan and practitioners must provide public relations professionals with the ideas, as well as the messages, you want to communicate. You probably will have to help them look for the best placements, too. Successful advertising involves extensive planning by agency people. The focus is on the longer term: the firm's position five years from now.

*Public Relations Activities Can Be Low in Cost.* Many public relations activities can be run quite economically. A seminar on tax legislation, a breakfast with speaker, a reception to honor a visiting dignitary—these are just a few examples of events costing only several hundred dollars but offering opportunities for returns.

*Public Relations People Deliver Contacts.* A public relations firm delivers three important ingredients: planning; introductions to influential people, including the press; and writing skills. The optimal mix of these ingredients, from an accounting firm's perspective, is 10 percent planning, 40 percent contacts, and 50 percent writing skills, but this mix is rare. The usual mix is 1 percent planning, 80 percent contacts, and 19 percent writing skills.

*Local Public Relations Firms Serve Offices Well.* If a firm has several offices spread geographically, a local public relations firm can help the office communicate with the local market better than a public relations firm in some distant location. There is no such thing as a national agency in public relations. Although they present themselves as linked into a network, the reality is that a public relations firm in New York or Washington handles the national media. In New York, its staff will deal with all the major trade publications, as well as *The New York Times* and the *Wall Street Journal*. In Washington, the staff will deal with the *Washington Post* and various association publications.

If your accounting firm is national, you will want representation on the West Coast, probably Los Angeles and San Francisco. Other cities that can be important for national, and many regional, accounting firms are Dallas, Chicago, Houston, and Philadelphia. Most regional firms and local offices of national firms are not striving for national coverage, although they certainly would welcome it. They really want to focus on the local market.

If your marketing management must choose between advertising and public relations, our view is that public relations efforts yield immediate results at lower costs. In addition, a public relations professional can introduce your firm's partners to influential members of the business and cultural community. However, first you must define a set of short- and long-term goals to help you measure the overall success of the programs you establish. The implication is not that public relations should supplant advertising. Some of us prefer the discipline of working with an advertising agency and using its people to direct our public relations efforts.

## Communication + Education = Mutual Understanding

Advertising people understand the public's frame of mind and know how to help accounting firms present their messages to the public. To date, however, the profession's attempts at advertising have been limited and generally uninteresting. In large part, this results from the lack of understanding on each side about the other. Accountants do not understand the discipline of advertising, and advertising people have assumed they could transfer their success with consumer goods to the specialized needs of professional service firms.

If accountants are going to work with advertising people successfully, the initiative probably will have to come from the agency people. In educating accountants about advertising, they will have to develop guidelines that direct the process for accountants. In addition to being students, accountants will have to teach advertising people about the unique characteristics of their firm—the business, its range of services, strengths and weaknesses, and client base. Only when this open communication occurs will there be the constructive relationship that is basic to excellent advertising programs.

## STRANGE BEDFELLOWS: HOW TO WORK SUCCESSFULLY WITH AN ADVERTISING AGENCY
*Robert J. Killian*
*Bozell, Jacobs, Kenyon & Eckhardt, Chicago*

Accounting firms and advertising agencies are just becoming acquainted, somewhat warily. Neither group is sure how the advertising of professional services will evolve.

The common complaint among accountants is, "Agencies don't understand our business." And it's true. Agencies do not. For starters, it is much easier to sell a product than a service. Advertising people know how to sell products very well. It is infinitely easier to sell a soft drink than a hotel. To take it one step further—and going to professional services is quite a large step—it is much easier to sell a hotel room than accounting or legal services. We are pioneers together in advertising professional services.

Also, accountants complain that agencies assign junior staff to their work. What accountants do not realize is that substantial accounting firms are still relatively small-budget advertisers. So misfits occur, caused by the misapplied logic: "We're a Big Eight firm. We should talk to one of the Top 20 agencies." That prestige-oriented selection process leaves a firm as one of its agency's smaller advertisers, and the top creative people apply their talents to larger accounts.

There is a structural problem built in for the agency, too. Accountants are successful, intelligent professional people. Partners are also very autonomous. What is the net result? They are terrible clients.

Why? Partners, like everyone else in the world, believe that they are advertising experts, and they bring this expertise to a committee structure in order to achieve consensus without surrendering autonomy. To date, this committee approach has resulted in advertising by accounting firms that is timid and tentative, bland and grey. It is also unfocused, with a typical message reading: "We are a full-service firm, and we offer all these services. Let us tell you about all of them."

The agency people know that accounting firms need their expertise, and accountants are beginning to realize that good advertising people can help firms reach their markets. But how do they get together? The process of finding an agency and building a collaborative effort is not easy. Advertising is both an art and a science, with a little bit of alchemy thrown in. There is no certification, and the range of skills is broad. However, a firm that does its homework can find the right agency to develop advertising that opens a dialogue with prospective clients and that presells for the firm's professionals.

In the following sections, I will outline key factors in selecting an agency and in solidifying the firm-agency relationship. Also described is the approval process, which is tangential to the relationship. Finally, 11 points underpinning successful advertising campaigns are presented.

## How to Choose an Advertising Agency: Eight Steps

Partners in an accounting firm are very familiar with selection processes. They go through a similar process with many potential clients every year. Selecting an advertising agency puts the accounting firm in the client role, but now the firm is the selector. The firm-agency relationship is a close one, and the selection process should be well thought out. Eight key points should be considered in formulating your firm's selection process.

*Buy Brains, Not Samples.* When an advertising campaign catches your (and everyone else's) attention, it can be tempting to conclude that the agency behind the campaign is the one for your firm. That conclusion may not be warranted. First, the people who created that campaign may have left the agency. Second, if they still work at the agency, you have no assurance that they would work on your project or campaign.

*Meet the Team.* Meet the people who will work directly with you. Especially important is the choice of the agency's account executive, the point man who will work with you every day. Look for—in fact, insist on—a spirit of partnership. Look for an advertising agency you can relate to in the same way you want to have clients relate to you. As an accountant, you do not want to be a vendor to your clients. You want to be a partner, an objective outside resource who comes in to help a client solve problems. Find advertising people who will fill this role for your firm.

*Look for a People Fit.* Look for people with whom you feel comfortable. Do not feel that it is unsophisticated or unprofessional to search for people with whom you work well. Developing an advertising campaign involves many hours of hard work from both organizations. The issues will change; the strategy will change; the situations will change; your objectives will change. But the people are constant. If you are comfortable with the agency's people, you will be able to adapt. This factor is very important.

*Find a Well-Run Agency.* You want an agency that is profitable and businesslike. Preferably it is one that is growing, too. It should be attracting new business from long-term and new clients.

***Look for Enthusiasm.*** If you want to find out how enthusiastic the agency people are about your business—and, indeed, how enthusiastic they are about their own—find out the agency's office hours. Show up, uninvited, a half-hour before the office opens or a half-hour after it closes. See who is still there. What are they doing? This visit (a surprise audit) can be eye-opening.

***Buy Independence.*** Assume that you are the partner in charge of marketing in a small accounting firm in Pittsburgh and that you sign up with the Pittsburgh branch of a New York agency. Everything goes well for a year. Then the New York agency obtains a larger accounting firm with a Pittsburgh office as a client. What happens? You are out of luck. In fact, you must start the process all over again. Independence can be key to maintaining your momentum. Engage an agency that can make a commitment to your firm.

***Find the Right Size.*** Size is a critical factor. Just as most accounting firms match their clients in size, an accounting firm should find an advertising agency that is the right size. There are only two important questions related to size. First, is the agency big enough to have all the resources your firm needs? Your firm may need help with brochures, direct mail, trade show exhibits, or some other service beyond print advertising. Find out if the agency can help you with the right resources.

Second, will your firm be a significant piece of the agency's business? The amount of care you will receive is proportional to your billings. It has happened that the chairman of a Big Eight firm has been told by an advertising executive, "I'm sorry, but you just don't spend enough for our top creative people to work on your account." That reaction can be upsetting.

How do you find the right fit? As a rule of thumb, your advertising billings should represent somewhere between 2 and 15 percent of the agency's income. On the one hand, you cannot expect the attention you want, "the A Team," if your work accounts for only one percent of the agency's business. On the other hand, if your account is more than 15 percent of its income, you are looking at much too small an agency.

*Talk to Their Clients.* Look at the agency's client list to find a service business or two. You probably will find a financial organization, perhaps a bank. Call your counterpart in that organization, and take that person to a leisurely, expensive lunch. Over lunch you should grill your counterpart to find out exactly what the working agency relationship is like. This is a small investment to learn about the quality and responsiveness of the agency's services.

## Six Factors in Working Together Successfully

Your firm has gone through a rigorous selection process, and both the firm and agency principals have toasted a long and mutually satisfying relationship. How can you solidify that relationship and really make it work? Six points form the foundation of a successful relationship.

*Be a Model Client.* If you are an accountant, you know that you have good clients and bad clients. The "good clients" tend to treat you as a valuable, independent resource. Your advertising team must serve in the same way—an objective, outside resource to you, the client. The key people in your firm must be available, information must be accessible, and your firm's staff must work to build a good working relationship with the agency's staff. Your firm and your agency must be partners.

*Sign a Multiyear Contract.* Long-term contracts are rare in advertising. If your firm can make this commitment, you will obviously make the agency's management very happy. But, more importantly, they will interpret your willingness as a desire for a stable relationship, something that can be very important to both your organizations.

*Be a Profitable Client.* Advertising agencies and accounting firms share at least one characteristic: They do not like to lose money. Unprofitable clients get short shrift. Insist that your firm's work be profitable in order to keep the agency's management from losing interest, or even resigning. At a minimum, less expensive, junior people will be assigned to an unprofitable account. Whether you work out a fee arrangement by the project or the hour, or on a retainer basis, profitability ensures the best work from your agency.

*Insist on Top-Quality Production Values.* What are production values? Printing, photography, typesetting, and all the other processes involved in turning out the final product are production values. If your advertising includes photographs, insist on the best photographers. Printers and typesetters vary enormously in quality; get the best. If your firm's work includes broadcast, invest in the best writing and production team.

You must have the best quality—which is expensive—because your firm is a professional organization and its advertising must be consistent with that professional image. To buy production services on the basis of price alone can and will make your firm look less than professional.

*Quantify Your Objectives.*   This point relates to any advertiser, but for accounting firms it contains a bit of irony. An accounting firm lives and dies by numbers, yet it is apparently very difficult to develop more than some vague generalizations of the firm's objectives.

Quantifying objectives allows a firm to measure its performance. Benchmark research will give you information about where your firm is today. Periodic testing—quarterly, semiannually, or annually—will allow your firm and your agency to measure your progress.

*Centralize.* The success of an advertising campaign depends in large part on the consistency of the image the firm portrays. However, partners and managers frequently have a high degree of autonomy, and it is not unusual for a brochure or newsletter to be produced without the knowledge of anyone else in the firm. This problem increases geometrically in the firm having multiple offices. Thus, autonomy can work against an advertising campaign. How you deal with this problem depends on you.

Minimally, an educational process would help everyone to know about the advertising campaign and its goals. The partner in charge of the advertising program (*not* a lower-level coordinator) might provide resources to help make a new promotional piece consistent with the firm's objectives. Budgetary and expenditure controls may be needed, too, according to the size and complexity of your organization.

## Nine Rules to Get the "Okay"

Your firm's team and the agency team are working together on a major campaign. One area can make or break that campaign. A structured approval process, during which key people sign off on the work, must be in place if a firm's campaign is to be successful.[3] This point is especially important in the partnership structure of an accounting firm where there could be 5, 23, or 722 partners who want to be involved in this exciting area. In the absence of an approval structure, a firm's campaign could be two to three years in approval.

If a firm cannot implement an approval structure that works, it should not be involved in advertising. The following nine rules provide a roadmap.

*Define the Process—in Writing.* The approval process should be developed early, taking recognition of a firm's special requirements. For example, a firm may require legal review of any communication to the public. The approval process should be written down so that everyone involved understands the process and can plan for contingencies (e.g., vacations, to avoid bottlenecks). This advance planning avoids the bottlenecks and infighting associated with many *ad hoc* committees. Having the process in writing helps everyone understand the process and allows them to keep a copy on file.

*Minimize the Number of Approvers.* In the best of all possible worlds, the final approval should come from two people—three, at most. In addition to saying "No," the approvers must be able to say, "Yes." What about all the other people in the firm who want to be part of the process? Their involvement should come in the front-end planning at the goal- and strategy-setting stages. Approval by committee, in the experience of most advertising executives, results in advertising that is routine and bland. Firms making the resource investment good advertising requires should get a more imaginative return on that investment.

*Stick to the Firm's Strategy.* A team of firm and agency representatives spent many hours establishing the firm's strategy. Keep that strategy in mind at all times. It is very easy, particularly when there is an *ad hoc* approval process, for a whim to appear attractive. It sometimes happens that a partner becomes involved late in the game and announces, "That's not the way we've always done things around here." Your firm may, however, have a new strategy. Stay on track.

*Circulate an Untouched Original.* When a photocopy of an advertisement is being circulated for comments or approval, attach an untouched original so that the changes, or "damage," can be tracked, particularly by the final approvers. Asking for suggested changes and explanations on a separate sheet, with signature, can cut down on the number of stylistic preferences suggested. The partner who wants to change "professionals" to "accountants, auditors, and consultants" will have a good reason if he must write an explanation. Also, the final approvers then see new ideas in addition to the changes made by subordinates, who know the approvers' personal preferences.

*Obtain Date and Time of Sign-Offs.* A person's initials usually indicate a sign-off. Having the date and time as well provides useful information for refining the approval process. For example, a bottleneck may have occurred because the copy did not make an interoffice overnight mail pouch; a 2 P.M. sign-off deadline could have been used to avoid that situation.

*Suggest Changes that Simplify.* The best advertising is simple, clear, uncomplicated. The best editors and copywriters are people who subtract. If copy needs to be changed, a useful discipline is to keep the same word length as the original. Changes made by firm personnel should be "suggested changes"; someone at the agency may be able to improve on the revision. If a significant change is requested by the firm because of a misunderstanding or an error by agency personnel, an explanation should accompany the change so that the same mistake will not be made on the next assignment.

*Stick to Your Specialty.* Approvers should understand their role in the approval process, and perform the appropriate functions. The person in charge of graphic standards should review an advertisement for graphic standards, not for legal implications. The tax consultant should review an advertisement for technical accuracy, not for stylistic suggestions. Again, advertising by committee yields weak results.

*Write Down Your Firm's Unwritten Rules.* Every firm has unwritten rules, both rational and irrational. The managing partner may hate the color brown. Titles are used in firm publications, but not on business cards. Writing these rules on paper for your agency may lead to some in-firm discussions about the need to maintain some of these rules and, perhaps, to change. However, if you let the agency staff know these rules, it can save considerable time and frustration for both the agency and the firm.

*Identify the Symptoms, Not the Cure.* It is very important for the firm's team to communicate to the agency what the advertisement is or is not communicating, as opposed to how it should be changed. For example, if your advertisement describes a computer-related seminar your firm is having in four weeks, you might tell the agency that the graphics are not eye-catching enough to draw the reader's attention. Your role is not to suggest an alternative, although the agency people may ask you for ideas. Your role is to provide creative direction, that is, to describe the gap between the advertisement's intent and the drafted advertisement. The creative team's role is to find the solution that fills that gap.

## Eleven Tips for Successful Advertising

Selecting the agency, developing a constructive relationship with the agency team, and implementing an approval process will take your firm well into its advertising program. There are some principles that form the underpinnings of successful advertising. They are also points that should be understood by your firm's partners and marketing professionals.

*Identify Your Firm's "Positioning Gap."* By position, we mean how your market perceives your firm today. That perception can be very different from the way your firm intends to portray itself. The distance between these two measurable points—the perception the market has today and the desired perception —is the ground your marketing effort must cover. Professionally conducted research can establish benchmarks to identify your starting point. Your goal then is to reach that desired position through consistent and effective marketing programs.

*Open a Dialogue.* Many accountants have the misconception that their firm must be perceived as unique. They believe their firm must offer something that their competitors do not. The simple truth is that you do not need to be unique—or better. Of course, you can exploit a unique advantage if one exists, provided that uniqueness is meaningful to your audience. There is no need, though, to invent an artificial position for the sake of appearance.

You must, however, convince your firm's prospects that your partners and staff are responsible, trustworthy, approachable professional people. The key point is to start a dialogue with the potential client. Portray your firm the way you want to be perceived, and communicate that message consistently.

You do not have to promise the moon; in fact, you must not. Your firm's message cannot be in any way misleading or dishonest. If, as tax consultants, you promise that an investment of $2,000 in an IRA will make someone 52 years old a millionaire, that is reprehensible. It also is not necessary.

***Adopt a Corporate Identity.*** An accounting firm must have a consistent corporate identity reflecting the dignity of the profession. A firm cannot run crowded, hard-to-read, ill-prepared, or inconsistent messages. This extends all the way from envelopes and business cards to advertising and public relations. In fact, anything that has the firm's name on it should be graphically consistent and communicate something positive about your firm. If your firm does not have a corporate graphic standards manual, start one tomorrow.

A corporate identity gives a firm a consistent personality. Some people would call an accounting firm having a personality a contradiction in terms, but that is not true. A review of a vertical trade publication, for instance, in health care, shows a growing number of accounting firms which are advertising. Comparison of their advertisements indicates that they are all very different. They communicate different firm personalities, sometimes, admittedly, bland. Advertisements should differ among firms, but one firm's advertisements should be consistent.

***Advertising Is Cumulative.*** Establishing an identity in the marketplace takes a long time. A firm generally does not advertise on Tuesday and gain a new client on Wednesday. It is very important for professionals to understand that a 12-month or 52-week commitment is necessary for success.

This long-term investment contrasts with many firms' current marketing activities which yield a quick payout. A partner could give someone a business card at a civic luncheon one day and have him as a client the next. A firm could run a seminar on Thursday and obtain several clients within a week.

If a firm's partners cannot make the long-term commitment advertising requires, they should not advertise. This is one area where the timid, tentative approach does not work. A one-shot advertisement is a waste of your firm's money. Even running one advertisement four times a year in a single publication is a minimal effort because the public memory lasts about 30 days. Although there would be some equity accruing, it is not likely to be appreciable. An investment in advertising requires consistency and frequency.

*Campaigns Presell.* Advertisements do not sell anything, but campaigns will presell your firm. A campaign will make a firm's name familiar in a market and will open a dialogue with a prospect. For professional development to be effective, individuals will have to continue that dialogue to close the sale that advertising presold. Many accountants know advertising builds awareness; they have seen the local automobile dealers' results. Accountants and other professionals, however, are just learning about advertising's preselling role.

*Use Appropriate Media.* Professional firms routinely consider advertising in newspapers and business publications, even radio and television. Those media may be appropriate, assuming they are executed well. From time to time, however, someone in a firm suggests other media, including billboards, skywriting, and matchbook covers. They are not consistent with a professional image. Do not even consider them.

*Give a Campaign Enough Time.* If a campaign is working, stick with it. Too many campaigns are killed when they are just getting started. This is particularly true with less sophisticated advertisers, such as professional service firms. In part, this results because partners, who are new to the process, watch a campaign develop, from concept through execution. By the time the campaign actually runs, they know it too well and become restless to change prematurely. There is a need for an education process and for prudent counsel from the agency.

*Advertising Must Be Active.* People are passive. They do not need to hear an accounting firm's message—unless they just had a dispute with the Internal Revenue Service over taxes. A firm's message must break through to reach people. To do this, your advertising has to be active in some sense, with a clear call to action. For example, your firm may offer a brochure to anyone who mails in a completed coupon. Active advertising reaches a market.

***Advertising Is Logic-Plus.*** If a firm's advertising is logical and rational, something may still be missing. Very few purchases we make in our lifetime are entirely rational decisions. Certainly the selection of an accounting firm or an advertising agency is not based solely on logic. Advertising, to be effective, must appeal to people's emotions, too.

***Advertising Is Simple.*** Your firm cannot communicate complex messages in advertising. The message must be simple. In a campaign, it is possible to have one message for each of the separate advertisements and, thus, to accumulate a fairly complex message. But remember: Simplicity is always on the advertiser's side.

Simplicity helps to cut through the clutter. All of us see a great deal of advertising, so much so that it tends to blur. Even though a firm may not have a great deal of competition for its message in its category, everyone is communicating around and against the firm's message. A grey message does not cut through the clutter. A simple, clear advertisement stands out.

***Risk Failure.*** Accounting firms, until now, have been timid advertisers. Timid advertisers' messages are never active, do not cut through the clutter, and never say anything startling. To be a risk-taker, an accounting firm is going to have to give up its traditional decision-making approach: the committee. Committee thinking focuses on avoiding failure. Its decisions favor the dull and safe approach. In advertising, the only risk run by the committee is wasting the firm's money.

In contrast, it is safe to say that virtually all successful communications that have breakthrough power, that is, the power to turn somebody on, inevitably will turn somebody off. Most great advertisements are to some extent controversial. High-stimulus advertising will always seem too risky to some, and a committee will inevitably homogenize any effort approaching that kind of impact.

How can the committee members get involved? The appropriate roles for the partner group relate to market planning and strategy formulation. Once they have agreed on the firm's objectives and strategies, development of the advertising plan should be assigned to *one* partner with support from the firm's marketing professional. The firm that risks failure is more likely to achieve success.

## No "Quick Fix" by Advertising

Advertising can be a powerful vehicle for an accounting firm. In addition to building awareness, advertising can presell for the firm's professionals charged with developing the practice. However, given the evolving nature of professional services advertising, the decision to advertise carries with it a commitment to consistency, frequency, and high quality, as well as extensive involvement by a partner and other firm professionals in selecting an agency, building a relationship with its people, and implementing the internal support systems, such as the approval process. In order to be successful in advertising, accountants will have to change some of their traditional approaches, such as decisions by committee, and take more risks.

## ☐ ADVERTISING SUCCESS DEPENDS ON POSITIONING

One prerequisite of successful advertising, as described by Dunleavy and Killian, is the development process focusing on positioning research and planning. In fact, this development process applies to all your marketing communication efforts —public relations, brochures, and newsletters, as well as advertising. It is critical to understand your firm's position or image with clients and prospects. Only with this understanding can you manage the process of shifting their perceptions to the desired image. You can assess your current image through formal research, and you should obtain professional help for this assessment.

If your firm has engaged or is considering engaging marketing communication consultants (a public relations firm, an advertising agency, etc.), each consultant will tell you that its positioning research approach will serve all your communication needs. That probably is not so. Each communication specialty has its particular needs, and its research will be slanted toward those needs.

Your best source of an unbiased positioning research approach is a firm offering only market research services. Of course, if your marketing director has research expertise, he could design the study and purchase support services. Other sources of research services could be a nearby university's business school.

You may find yourself in the position of having to consider a proposal from a public relations firm or an advertising agency. Plead ignorance of research methods, and tell the supplier that you need an objective opinion. Then call in the market researcher. Why? Sound research allows you to develop workable strategies for your communications with clients, staff, referral sources, the media, and important others. You, then, would be basing a decision to advertise on hard data.

Certainly some firms are using advertising with success, usually as one aspect of a comprehensive marketing plan. Stephen Dietrich, who directed Peat Marwick's advertising efforts, described the results of that firm's industry-specific campaigns:

> We estimated that the three campaigns—running from April 1983, through December 1983—would yield fewer than 1000 responses. By July 1983, we had well over 2500 leads.[4]

Williams, Young & Associates, a Madison, Wisconsin firm, has had a good response to its full-page advertisements in the regional editions of *Time* and three other national weekly magazines.[5]

Once you decide that advertising supports your firm's

marketing plan, your advertising agency will help you decide whether to use print or electronic media. The agency will also help you evaluate choices within these categories, including:

| Print | Electronic |
| --- | --- |
| Newspapers—Local/national | Radio |
| Business publications— | Network television |
| Local/national | Cable television |
| Trade publications— | |
| Local/national | |
| Yellow pages | |
| Community organization | |
| programs | |

Differential cost and effectiveness data should support their recommendations.

Accounting firms certainly have marketing opportunities for which advertising is an appropriate tool. If your firm is going to use advertising effectively, you must understand the pros and cons of using this powerful tool.

## □ NOTES

1. Paul N. Bloom, "Effective Marketing for Professional Services," *Harvard Business Review* (September–October 1984): 107.
2. Thomas E. King and M. Robert Carver, Jr., "CPA Advertising: How Successful Has It Been?" *Financial Executive* (September 1984): 42.
3. See Robert J. Killian, "Getting Ads Approved Without Pain," *Advertising Age* (March 12, 1984): M-22.
4. Carole A. Congram, "The Role of the National Office in Marketing Accounting Services," in Thomas M. Bloch, Gregory D. Upah, and Valarie Zeithaml, eds., *Services Marketing in a Changing Environment; Proceedings of the AMA's Third Annual Services Marketing Conference* (Chicago: American Marketing Association, 1985): 88.
5. "Williams Young Enjoys National Advertiser Status at Regional Rates," *CPA Marketing Report* (December 1984): 6–8.

# PART THREE

# HOW TO POSITION FOR SUCCESS

# 6

# HOW VIABLE IS YOUR FIRM?

As competitive pressures mount, the long-term prospects for many firms diminish. Why? Accounting firms grow in relation to client growth, professional development opportunities, new service development, compensation, and profitability. Most firms which have a business planning process recognize this relationship. Their business plans comprise several growth strategies—some short-term, others long-term. However, these progressive firms are a small minority. Most firms continue to rely on short-term, quick-fix strategies.

Short-term strategies appear attractive because of their fast pay-off, but they must be complemented by other strategies for growth to continue. Merger is one example of a short-term strategy. The combination of two sole practitioners or two firms yields a high percentage revenue gain for one year, as well as one-time savings from consolidation. However, without additional strategies and plans, the combined firm's growth rate will approximate, at best, the premerger growth rate of the dominant practice. Many short-term strategies do attain growth. Few sustain growth. To sustain it, partner commitment is needed. Long-term marketing strategies must be adopted by the practice's management group if your firm is to achieve, control, and sustain high growth.

Accounting firms which achieve high growth over a five- to ten-year period have certain characteristics in common. In this chapter, Robert W. Denney, a marketing consultant who has worked with accounting firms of all sizes, describes the 10 characteristics of high-growth firms.

Your firm's management group can use Denney's list to evaluate your firm's growth posture by asking such questions as: Is the firm "our firm," or do the partners say "my firm"? Do we reward professionals for marketing activities? The answers will indicate the degree to which your firm is poised to meet market demands and to grow.

Denney contends that high-growth firms will be positioned to market "smarter," not "harder." After identifying these common characteristics successful firms share, he describes eight marketing-related areas which he believes will challenge the profession in the coming years. Meeting these challenges successfully requires that partners commit to achieving controlled and sustained growth.

---

## WE'VE ONLY JUST BEGUN, BUT WHERE DO WE GO FROM HERE?

*Robert W. Denney*
*Robert Denney Associates*

The juxtaposition of song titles is deliberate. Together, they describe aptly the current situation in accounting firms: The accounting profession has been marketing its services for 10 years. It has come a long way, but it has only just begun. So where does it go from here?

The firms that have succeeded so far in this increasingly competitive environment share certain characteristics, which are described in the following section. The firms that will grow and prosper in the years ahead must do more. They must move into other marketing areas and position themselves to better serve their clients. The areas that are paramount are discussed in the second section.

## Ten Characteristics of High-Growth Firms

In consulting with a broad range of accounting practices including local, regional, and national firms, we have noticed that certain characteristics recur across practices that experience high growth, one good criterion of success. The following 10 characteristics may vary in importance from firm to firm, but they all can be seen in the firm having high growth for several consecutive years, which, in our estimation, is the best predictor of success in the future.

*High-Growth Firms Are Team Thinkers.* A spirit of cooperation characterizes the high-growth firm. A partner in a high-growth firm talks about "our practice," not "my practice." That partner also asks, "How can we grow as a firm or an office so that we all advance professionally and earn more income?"

*High-Growth Firms Are Committed to Marketing.* Professionals in a successful, high-growth firm realize that marketing is an attitude that places the client first. That attitude is communicated by the partners to everyone in the firm. In a firm that has made a half-hearted commitment to marketing, little will be accomplished.

*High-Growth Firms Involve Everyone in Marketing.* Everyone in the firm must participate in the marketing effort: every partner, manager, staff person, secretary, telephone operator, receptionist, and mail person. Marketing is an attitude; in a high-growth firm, everyone has it.

*High-Growth Firms Know That Professionals Must Market Themselves.* Providers of a service must do much of the marketing of the service. Just as health care professionals must market themselves, so must accountants and consultants. Marketing professionals can help, but, in the end, the accountant and the consultant have to market and sell themselves and their services. In high-growth firms, the service providers accept marketing as their responsibility.

***High-Growth Firms Know That Marketing Means Hard Work.*** The professionals understand that marketing takes hard work. They understand that marketing involves planning, action, risk-taking, creativity, and learning new skills. In the process, these professionals find that the culture of their firm changes. Adapting to this evolving culture presents another challenge, which they accept.

***High-Growth Firms Treat Marketing Professionals as Part of the Team.*** In the high-growth firm, accountants welcome the assistance of marketing professionals. In any successful marketing activity, a marketing professional is part of the team—from the start.

***High-Growth Firms Experience Humility.*** Professionals in high-growth firms experience an unusually high degree of humility. These professionals realize that other accountants and consultants can do exactly what they do, perhaps just as well, and that marketing and service are necessary to distinguish a firm and to help it grow.

***High-Growth Firms Know That the Client Defines Quality.*** Many professionals believe that they define quality service. However, professionals in high-growth firms take a different position. They understand that the client's definition not only is more important, but also is what really matters.

***High-Growth Firms Reward Marketing.*** Partners and staff are compensated for results. Everyone understands that their marketing efforts are measured and that results count.

***High-Growth Firms Care about Their Image.*** Most professionals understand that marketing encompasses both current clients and new business. In high-growth firms, professionals also recognize the importance of a firm's image, that is, the reputation the firm or office projects to the broad outside world. High-growth firms want to know how they are perceived, and they continually monitor the perceptions of their publics.

These 10 characteristics indicate the extent to which firms have incorporated marketing into their operations. The percentage of accounting firms having all 10 characteristics is not nearly high enough. Certainly fewer than half have most of them, indicating that we have a long way to go.

## What Is the Outlook for Marketing Accounting Services?

Clients will continue "comparative shopping" as they look for service and value. As a result, competitive pressures will increase. In fact, they could increase at a faster pace than we have seen. These pressures will cause us to change, adapt, or create in eight significant areas.

*New Product Development Will Increase.* The accounting profession has been successful in identifying target markets. We have not been successful in developing services (i.e., pre-packaged products) to meet the needs of these target markets. There are a few obvious success stories, such as litigation support systems and inventory control systems for distributors. Management consultants have been instrumental in developing these service lines, but audit and tax professionals must also become involved in this activity. Marketing professionals will play a vital role in identifying new services and in institutionalizing these services within firms.

*Marketing Information Systems Will Be Developed.* In the next few years, we will see more requests for market research and, thus, the development of marketing information systems. Many accounting firms have not placed much emphasis on this area and, as a result, have not obtained reliable data to use in market planning. This situation will change as accountants and consultants realize the importance of surveying clients to identify services needed, expectations, and satisfaction levels.

*Requests for Proposals Will Increase.* There will be a continued increase in the number of proposals and presentations, formal or informal, to the smallest of prospective clients as well as to large corporate entities. It is important to understand the reasons for this increase because accountants find the proposal process difficult and tiring.

First, it is easy to say there are general trends for companies to have substantiating data and to contain costs. However, another reason is more critical and germane. For years the accounting profession has marketed its services, particularly audits, as commodities. Price-cutting, or low-balling, has been almost the only substantive marketing activity used by many firms, large and small. If your firm's services are commodities and price is the only difference, who can blame the prospective client for shopping around? In our experience, however, *clients would prefer to pay more if they were convinced they were really receiving benefits.*

Of course, some people will always buy on price. That is why discount stores have been successful. But it is interesting to note that, in the last few years, many retailers have come to realize that people want quality and will pay more for it. K Mart, Sears, and J. C. Penney are shifting their focus because shoppers are "trading up." These retailers know people will pay more if they get more. The accounting profession has been slow to recognize this desire for quality. As a result, we are going to be faced with more requests for proposals and presentations. Also, clients will ask more frequently what we have done for them and why the money they have spent with us has been well spent.

***Marketing Tools Will Require More Creativity.*** Accounting firms need better execution of all the marketing tools we are using: public relations, brochures, newsletters, advertising, personal selling. Once upon a time, a firm had an advantage with a brochure or newsletter, or an advertisement in a charity magazine or publication. Now many firms are using these tools, so the competitive edge is lost. Thus, more creative marketers are asking tougher questions: "How do I design better mailing pieces?" or "How do I develop brochures that stand out and really do define and market the firm?" We will have to do a better, more creative job of using marketing tools effectively.

***New Promotional Ideas Will Develop.*** In the early 1970s, it was unheard of for a firm to underwrite a program on public television. Today it is a common occurrence in most major cities. We need new, creative approaches for communicating with our audience—to carry the message about our firms, their services, and their people.

***The Account Executive Concept Will Be Adopted.*** What differentiates accounting professionals? Service—the way a professional delivers and markets a firm's services—is key. In accounting firms, we will see the development of the account executive concept: A partner will manage all aspects of the relationship with the client. Further, that partner may not perform any billable work.

Many law firms provide a model with the role of the responsible attorney. A responsible attorney identifies the client's needs, manages the relationship, administers and controls the work, and manages the people that are working with the client. This partner may not work on any specific legal matters, yet he will bill for the time involved. This concept will come to public accounting, although at this point it is foreign to most acountants.

***Women Will Play a Vital Role in Marketing.*** In both architectural and law firms, women have demonstrated their ability to market and to sell professional services. Architectural firms have had women in marketing and sales positions for over 10 years. They are better able than most of the men in the architectural field to market for architects and to define the project before introducing the professionals.

In the last decade, women who have become partners in law firms have been promoted not only for their technical competence, but also for their ability to attract and retain clients. Women—accounting and consulting professionals, marketing directors, and communication professionals—are superb in this area. Their role will become stronger in the coming years.

***The Role of Marketing Professionals Will Expand.*** Marketing professionals have two markets. First they have all the clients, prospects, and third parties, as well as the general public of the firm. That is almost the easier market with which to work. The second market consists of the firms themselves. We are the people who have made a commitment to marketing—to understand it better and to know the importance of it. By taking marketing positions as consultants, employees, or partners, we have assumed a responsibility to educate, train, goad, and cajole accountants and consultants until they understand marketing, until they embrace the attitude, and until they make the commitment to market. Marketing could be the key to survival for many firms, as it has been in the legal profession.

As firms become more marketing-oriented, marketing consultants will play more important roles. We will continue to write the brochures and newsletters. We will develop and implement reporting systems. But there are many marketing principles yet to be introduced into accounting firms. If a marketing activity or tool has not been proscribed or even considered, develop a plan and present it to the appropriate people. When we have their involvement and commitment, we become credible and invaluable. Then accountants and consultants become involved. As we in marketing assume leadership, we will be working *beside* the professionals, not *for* them.

Predicting the future can be dangerous, especially if people remember the predictions. However, competitive pressures will force firms to develop new services and to use marketing tools more effectively and creatively. At the same time, new professional opportunities will open up for both marketing and client service professionals.

We have only just begun—without doubt. However, we cannot sit back and congratulate ourselves on the road we have traveled. To borrow from a Chinese proverb, the journey of a few thousand miles begins with a few tiny steps, and we have taken only the first steps. There are many more steps, and the firms that are survivors understand the hard work, and the fun involved.

# ☐ THE MARKETING CHALLENGE

What's marketing? For professional service firms, marketing is the process of attracting, establishing, and reinforcing client relationships. In successful organizations, marketing is inextricably linked with business planning. Accounting firms that will grow and prosper understand the linkage; they are refining the process to fit the needs of their firms. If you and your partners want your firm to be a winner, accept these four challenges.

*Maintain and Expand Client Relationships.* To an accounting firm, clients are assets. Successful client retention programs are built on effective client service evolving from a client-centered philosophy. Effective client service drives a firm's image, attracts creative professionals, and promotes loyal, long-term client relationships. When a firm ignores client needs, it runs the risk of losing clients. Then, poor relationships become a liability which few firms can afford. Can yours?

*Adapt to Change.* The accounting profession is changing rapidly. Clients merge; firms merge. Advertising moves beyond the experimental stage. Congressmen question independence. The list could go on and on. In this pressured environment, some firms will not survive, especially those which remain technically oriented. Technical proficiency is necessary, but for clients it is not sufficient. Your firm's partners and professionals must understand not only technical matters, but also how technical expertise helps a client organization achieve its objectives. When professionals can take that step, they begin to shift toward a client-centered orientation.

*Be Accountable.* Marketing forces a firm to live up to its claims. How? One of the key elements in marketing is visibility. Accounting firms which run effective marketing programs are more visible in their markets. They have more opportunities to propose; increased opportunities should lead to new clients. If your marketing position stresses the importance of client needs and your firm's professionals and systems fail to be responsive to these needs, your firm's credibility will be questioned. Success demands accountability.

*Make a Commitment.* Integrating marketing into an organization with the traditions and complexities of an accounting firm is no easy task. While many firms have established a marketing function, they have not necessarily accepted and internalized the professionalism and the discipline of marketing. For the two disciplines to have a long-term relationship, it will take commitment, understanding, and trust from both sides. Marketers will need to study and understand the complex workings of and demands on accounting firms. Similarly, accountants must begin to listen to marketing professionals, as opposed to telling them what to do. Both accountants and marketers must work hard to define their roles and their working relationship in order to achieve results.

What is marketing? Marketing is one of the challenges of being a professional.

# THE MARKETING OF ACCOUNTING SERVICES: A SELECTED BIBLIOGRAPHY

*KENT WHEILER*
*Graduate School of Business*
*The University of Texas at Austin*

Axline, Larry L. 1984. Are your clients satisfied? *Journal of Accountancy* (July): 84–90.

Block, Max. 1980. Any limits to "marketing" CPA services? *The CPA Journal* (August): 35–40.

Bloom, Paul N. 1977. Advertising in the professions: the critical issues. *Journal of Marketing* (July): 103–110.

Braun, Irwin. 1981. *Building a Successful Professional Practice With Advertising*. New York: AMACOM.

Braun, Irwin. 1982. Seven major mistakes accountants make in advertising. *The CPA Journal* (January): 82–83.

Carpenter, Susan R. Whisnant. 1983. *Marketing CPA Services,* The Foundation for Accounting Education.

Carver, M. Robert, Jr., Thomas E. King and Wayne A. Label. 1979. Clients' views of the consequences of advertising by accountants. *Journal of Accountancy* (September): 113–115.

Carver, M. Robert, Jr., Thomas E. King and Wayne A. Label. 1979. Attitudes toward advertising by accountants. *Financial Executive* (October): 27–32.

Casavant, Richard. 1981. Practice development: a marketing approach. *The Accountants Digest* (June): 203–206.

Chase, Richard B. 1978. Where does the customer fit in a service operation? *Harvard Business Review* (November–December): 137–142.

Churchill, Gilbert A. 1979. *Marketing Research: Methodological Foundations*. Hinsdale, IL: Dryden Press.

Cypert, Samuel. 1984. How to produce an effective firm brochure. *Practical Accountant* (February): 79–84.

Danos, Paul and David Shields. 1981. Referrals from bankers and attorneys. *The CPA Journal* (May): 13–19.

Darling, John R. 1977. Attitudes toward advertising by accountants. *Journal of Accountancy* (February): 48–53.

Denney, Robert W. 1983. *Marketing Accounting Services.* New York: Van Nostrand Reinhold Company, Inc.

Denney, Robert W. 1981. How to develop—and implement—a marketing plan for your firm. *Practical Accountant* (July): 18–29.

Dumesic, Ruth J. and Neil M. Ford. 1982. Internal practice development: an overlooked strategy for marketing professional services. *Practical Accountant* (December): 39–44.

Eisenberg, Ted. 1982. Tips on how to prepare an effective firm brochure. *Practical Accountant* (June): 29–32.

Erdos, Paul L. 1970. *Professional Mail Surveys.* New York: McGraw-Hill Inc.

Gatton, J. Patrick and Robert E. Schlosser. 1982. Helping staff members sell your firm's services. *Practical Accountant* (October): 63–67.

George, William R. and Leonard L. Berry. 1981. Guidelines for the advertising of services. *Business Horizons* (July–August): 52–56.

George, William R. and Richard M. Murray. 1975. Marketing practices of CPA firms. *The CPA Journal* (October): 33–36.

George, William R. and Paul J. Solomon. 1980. Marketing strategies for improving practice development. *Journal of Accountancy* (February): 79–84.

Gotlieb, Jerry B. and Bill N. Schwartz. 1982. How a CPA firm can analyze the market for its services. *Ohio CPA Journal* (Winter): 11–15.

Gummesson, Evert. 1981. The marketing of professional services—25 propositions. In *Marketing of Services,* eds. James H. Donnelly and William R. George, pp. 108–112. Chicago: American Marketing Association.

Hall, Richard C. 1982. How to expand your services to clients—and build your practice. *Practical Accountant* (March): 53–59.

Hanggi, Gerald A. 1980. Media advertising as a practice development tool. *Journal of Accountancy* (January): 54–58.

Hoffman, Arthur W. 1981. How advertising helped a new CPA firm build its practice. *Practical Accountant* (October): 52–56.

Holder, Will, Adel El-Ansary and Beverly Kooi. 1981. Professional service marketing to the federal government: marketing conditions and implications to marketing strategies. In *Marketing of Services,* eds. James H. Donnelly and William R. George, pp. 91–94. Chicago: American Marketing Association.

Kessler, Ellen Terry. 1981. Advertising accounting services: how effective has it been? *Practical Accountant* (July): 37–44.

Kotler, Philip and Paul N. Bloom. 1984. *Marketing Professional Services.* Englewood Cliffs, N.J.: Prentice-Hall, Inc.

Kotler, Philip and Richard A. Connor, Jr. 1977. Marketing professional services. *Journal of Marketing* (January): 71–76.

Larkin, Joseph J. and Marcia B. Sherwood. 1981. Strategic marketing of public accounting services. *The CPA Journal* (September): 46–51.

Levitt, Theodore. 1972. Production-line approach to service. *Harvard Business Review* (September–October): 41–52.

Levitt, Theodore. 1976. The industrialization of service. *Harvard Business Review* (September–October): 63–74.

Mahon, James J. 1982. *The Marketing of Professional Accounting Services: A Personal Practice Development Approach.* New York: John Wiley & Sons.

Marcus, Bruce W. 1981. What you should know about marketing accounting services. *Practical Accountant* (October): 48–51.

Maxey, Richard D. 1983. How to plan an advertising campaign. *Practical Accountant* (December): 59–61.

Meiners, Gerard J. 1981. A local CPA firm's experiences with advertising. *Practical Accountant* (July): 45–48.

Moldenhauer, C. A. 1982. How to sell consulting services. *Journal of Small Business Management* (April): 25–27.

Murray, Richard M. 1982. A growth plan for smaller accounting firms. *Practical Accountant* (May): 69–71.

Murray, Richard M. and William R. George. 1979. Managing CPA personnel—a marketing perspective. *The CPA Journal* (July): 17–22.

Netterville, Jake L. 1983. Practicing practice development: 13 proven techniques. *Practical Accountant* (August): 81–85.

Nykiel, Kenneth J. 1982. How to develop—and implement—a successful marketing plan. *Practical Accountant* (May): 37–41.

Ostlund, A. Clayton. 1978. Advertising—in the public interest? *Journal of Accountancy* (January): 59–63.

Piaker, Phillip M. 1980. Dealing with competition. *The CPA Journal* (October): 5–9.

Rachlin, Norman S. 1983. *Eleven Steps to Building a Profitable Accounting Practice.* McGraw-Hill Book Company.

Rachlin, Norman S. 1984. Is there (enough) life after the tax season? *Journal of Accountancy* (April): 68–76.

Rachlin, Norman S. 1979. A "general ledger" referral system for building your practice. *Practical Accountant* (October–November): 43–46.

Raimond, Paul. 1983. Marketing your firm: solve the identity puzzle first. *Accountancy* (September): 128–130.

Rathmell, John M. 1974. *Marketing in the Service Sector.* Cambridge, MA: Winthrop Publishers, Inc.

Retterer, Jack. 1983. How to develop your selling and marketing skills. *Practical Accountant* (February): 45–49.

Sasser, W. Earl. 1976. Match supply and demand in service industries. *Harvard Business Review* (November–December): 133–140.

Schwersenz, Jack. 1979. Marketing your services. *The CPA Journal* (October): 11–15.

Scott, Richard A. and Donna H. Rudderow. 1983. Advertising by accountants: how clients and practitioners feel about it. *Practical Accountant* (April): 71–76.

Sellers, James H. and Paul J. Solomon. 1978. CPA advertising: opinions of the profession. *Journal of Accountancy* (February): 70–77.

Siegel, Gary and James P. Martin. 1978. The need for national institutional advertising. *The CPA Journal* (April): 27–30.

Skigen, Michael R. 1981. Advertising on a limited budget: a small firm's experience. *Practical Accountant* (October): 57–61.

Smith, Bradford E. 1980. Reaching the public: the CPA's new image. *Journal of Accountancy* (January): 47–52.

Solomon, Paul J. and James H. Sellers. 1978. Advertising and the accounting profession: an empirical analysis. In *Research Frontiers in Marketing: Dialogues and Directions,* ed. Subhash C. Jain, pp. 285–287. Chicago: American Marketing Association.

Stevens, Mark. 1981. *The Big Eight.* New York: Macmillan Publishing Co.

Stiff, Ronald. 1976. The changing role of professional service marketing. In *Marketing: 1776–1976 and Beyond,* ed. Kenneth L. Bernhardt, pp. 283–286. Chicago: American Marketing Association.

Stiff, Ronald. 1977. CPA attitudes toward marketing communications. In *Contemporary Marketing Thought,* eds. Barnett A. Greenberg and Danny N. Bellenger, pp. 31–33. Chicago: American Marketing Association.

Stiff, Ronald. 1981. The effects of marketing activities on the quality of professional services. In *Marketing of Services.* eds. James H. Donnelly and William R. George, pp. 78–81. Chicago: American Marketing Association.

Stover, Beryl C. Argall. 1981. Firm brochures and client newsletters—two vital marketing tools. *Practical Accountant* (July): 30–36.

Thomas, Dan R. E. 1978. Strategy is different in service businesses. *Harvard Business Review* (July–August): 158–165.

Turner, Everett B. 1969. Marketing professional services. *Journal of Marketing* (October): 56–61.

Upah, Gregory D. and Ernest B. Uhr. 1981. Advertising by public accountants: a review and evaluation of copy strategy. In *Marketing of Services,* eds. James H. Donnelly and William R. George, pp. 95–98. Chicago: American Marketing Association.

Webb, Stan G. 1982. *Marketing and Strategic Planning for Professional Service Firms.* New York: AMACOM.

Weinstein, Stephen. 1983. Marketing accounting services: what's happening today (and tomorrow) and what you can do about it. *Practical Accountant* (September): 73–82.

Wheatley, Edward W. 1983. *Marketing Professional Services.* Englewood Cliffs, NJ: Prentice-Hall, Inc.

Wheatley, Edward W. 1983. Auditing your marketing performance. *Journal of Accountancy* (September): 68–75.

Williams, Albert S. 1983. Starting a CPA firm. *Journal of Accountancy* (June): 80–86.

Wilson, Aubrey. 1972. *The Marketing of Professional Services.* London: McGraw-Hill Book Company (UK).

Wittreich, Warren J. 1966. How to buy/sell professional services. *Harvard Business Review* (March–April): 127–138.

Wood, Thomas D. and Donald A. Bill. 1978. New Rule 502 and effective advertising by CPAs. *Journal of Accountancy* (June): 65–70.

Zuckert, Donald M. 1977. Think about your advertising program. *The CPA Journal* (October): 11–13.

# APPENDIX: SEMINAR SITE CHECKLIST

Many accounting firms have used the seminar as a public relations activity with clients and prospective clients, as well as with referral sources. The details involved are too numerous to count, but every experienced seminar planner has a story to tell about the forgotten detail that did count. The most successful seminars are well planned, and a good checklist is a valuable tool for planning.

The following checklist serves as a starting point for tailoring a list to your firm's needs. If many of your firm's seminars (or other events) are similar, you will probably have a tailored list after one or two events. By using the checklist, you can review the various areas that need to be covered and then delegate responsibility more effectively.

1. *Location*:

   Easily accessible                          ( )

   Adequate transportation                    ( )

   Taxis readily available                     ( )

   Plenty of free parking                      ( )

   Neighborhood OK                            ( )

   Stores and restaurants nearby               ( )

2. *Property*

    Attractive inside and out                        ( )

    Bedroom clean, attractive                    ( )

    Air-conditioned                               ( )

3. *Meeting Room(s)*:

    Enough available for both general and group
sessions    ( )

    Convenient locations    ( )

    Separate air-conditioning/heat controls    ( )

    Size of general meeting room
L ___ W ___ H ___

    Size of audience the room can accommodate    _____

    Schoolroom style, with tables, paper and pens    ( )

    U-shaped conference    ( )

    Theater style    ( )

    Head table for how many    _____

    Room big enough without crowding    ( )

    Space inside or adjacent for:

        Coffee break    ( )

    Registration table    ( )

    Name badges    ( )

    List of attendees    ( )

    Noise:

        None    ( )

        From adjoining room    ( )

    Room lighting adequate    ( )

    Lighting controlled by:

        One switch    ( )

        Several switches    ( )

    Lighting controls:

        In room    ( )

        Just outside    ( )

Elsewhere ( )

Room can be blacked out ( )

Electrical outlets convenient for projectors ( )

Heavy-duty cord needed ( )

Position tape recorder near lectern ( )

Master switch easily installed at projection
table or lectern ( )

Room available when ———

Is there another event immediately preceding
seminar ( )

What, and when scheduled out ———

Our equipment can be set up night before
A.M. meeting or morning before P.M. meeting ( )

Local staff help available ( )

Room will serve for both general meeting and
luncheon/dinner ( )

Deadline hour for recessing ———

Above checks made, as appropriate, in group
session rooms ( )

Location of rest rooms ( )

Location of public phones ( )

4. *Public Address and Projection Facilities*:

PA system is:

   Self-contained ( )

   Built-in around room ( )

Will tape recorder tie into it ( )

Lectern mikes or on table ( )

Stand mikes ( )

Lavalier mikes ( )

House engineer available if needed ( )

System checked for acoustics,
reverberations, clarity ( )

Projection screen is:

   Built-in                                                    ( )

   Pull-down                                       ( )

   Portable and available                 ( )

Projection screen size: _____

Screen clean, in good shape            ( )

Ceiling high enough for $6' \times 6'$ or $8' \times 8'$
screen plus tripod or other stand     ( )

5. *Luncheon/Dinner Room*:

PA and projection, lighting and controls, air-conditioning and heat controls, noise and acoustics factors checked            ( )

Menu _____

Seating—number needed

   At round tables                  ____

   At square tables                ____

   At rectangular tables          ____

   At U-shaped setup             ____

Total capacity needed              ____

Tables to be numbered             ____

Numbers and display stands available  ____

Head table elevated                ( )

Platform steady, secure           ( )

Noise deadening cover             ( )

Place settings—number needed    ____

Lectern with minimum top of $17 \times 22$ inches  ( )

Lectern lighted and working        ( )

   Separate circuit from other room lights  ( )

   Own switch                    ( )

   Set up before meal             ( )

   After meal                      ( )

Number of waiters assigned to function          ____

Name of person in charge                        _____

6. *Organization for Receptions, Meals, Breaks*:

Private bar wanted                              (  )

If available, locate where                      _____

We pay:

By drink                                        (  )

By bottle                                       (  )

(If latter and we pay for any bottle opened, unused contents ours; used for hospitality.)

Selected liquors                               (  )

or a complete stock                            (  )

Elaborate appetizers                           (  )

or peanuts/chips                               (  )

Separate premeal reception for honored guests. If so:

Private suite                               (  )

Adjacent room                               (  )

Other                                       (  )

Arrangements for water and glasses             (  )

Refreshments                                   (  )

Firm understanding about service: when delivered, replenished, removed and quantity     (  )

7. *Special Arrangements, Equipment*:

Place cards:                                   (  )

Head table                                  (  )

Other tables                                (  )

"Table tents" with legends for special tables (such as Press)                                 (  )

Flowers:                                       (  )

Head table                                  (  )

| | |
|---|---|
| Other tables | ( ) |
| Favors | ( ) |
| Commercial souvenirs allowed on tables or chairs | ( ) |
| Movie projector(s) needed in | ( ) |
|     Dining room | ( ) |
|     General meeting room | ( ) |
|     Group session rooms | ( ) |
|     16mm | ( ) |
|     or Super—8mm | ( ) |
|     Tested and working | ( ) |
|     Take-up reels | ( ) |
|     Spare lamps | ( ) |
|     Sound | ( ) |
|     or silent | ( ) |
| Slide projector(s) needed in | ( ) |
|     Dining room | ( ) |
|     General meeting room | ( ) |
|     Group session rooms | ( ) |
|     Tested and working | ( ) |
|     Remote control | ( ) |
|     Remote extension | ( ) |
|     Focus from remote | ( ) |
|     Sound or silent | ( ) |
|     Spare lamps | ( ) |
| Number of tape recorders needed to cover all meetings | _____ |
| Tested, working | ( ) |
|     New tapes | ( ) |
|     Extension speakers needed | ( ) |
| How about: Easels | ( ) |
|     Blackboard | ( ) |
|     Chalk, eraser | ( ) |

Flannel boards                                      ( )
Extension cords                                     ( )
Portable screens                                    ( )
Stand podium lighted and working                    ( )
Stand or PA mike tested and working                 ( )
How many and where                                  ⎯⎯⎯

8. *Billing, Check-Out*:
   Have firm billing arrangements been made
   with management                                  ( )
   Is there a written agreement on items guests
   may charge                                       ( )
   Liberal charge privileges for host personnel     ( )
   Check-out time                                   ⎯⎯⎯
   Can be extended to ⎯⎯ if absolutely necessary

9. *General Premeeting and Conference
   Checkpoints*:
   First notice of meeting mailed                   ⎯⎯
   Follow-up notice sent                            ⎯⎯
   Conference or press kits                         ⎯⎯
   Registration cards                               ⎯⎯
   Who's at registration table                      ⎯⎯
   Name tags for delegates and guests               ⎯⎯
      Made ahead                                    ( )
      Take blanks, markers                          ( )
   Advance program or agenda                        ( )
   Photographer lined up                            ( )
   Any special equipment needed                     ( )
   If "yes," what                                   ⎯⎯⎯
   Are easel signs in lobby needed to direct people ⎯⎯⎯

Will events be listed on announcements board
in lobby                                                          (   )
   Done        OK                                  _____

Facts for speaker introductions                                  (   )
If so, done                                                       (   )

Timetable needed                                                  (   )
Done                                                              (   )

Head table seating list                                          (   )
Done                                                              (   )

10. *Publicity*:

Advance release on meeting                                       (   )
If so, release date                                              _____

Advance release on major speeches                                (   )
If so, release date                                              _____

Advance copies of major speech texts                             (   )
If latter unavailable, on-the-spot release
arrangements OK and made                                         (   )

If pressroom desirable, arranged
   Near meeting rooms                               (   )

   Typewriters, copy paper, advance releases,
   coffee urn, telephone(s)                         (   )

   Copying machine needed                           (   )

   Who is assigned to press room                    _____

News conference for major speakers                               (   )

TV interviews                                                     (   )

Radio                                                             (   )

Hometown coverage for attendees, delegates,
speakers                                                          (   )

Follow-up news release on meeting                                (   )

Alternate                                                         _____

11. *Staff Assignments*:

Specific personnel assignments made for
handling projections, lighting control,

presentations, liaison with hotel management
VIPs, other duties                                      (  )
(Attach assignment list)

12. *VIP Treatment*:

Transportation for VIPs arranged in advance
to and from city                                        (  )

Arriving where and when (make notes below)

Departing where and when

Who's meeting VIPs

Also handling departures

Car rentals needed                                      (  )

We pay transportation                                   (  )

Mutually understood                                     (  )

Method mutually understood, too                         (  )

If spouses accompany any VIPs, is policy mutually understood re: charges and other costs           (  )

# INDEX